Captured Officers being escorted to the rear near Amman, passing a squadron of New Zealanders going into action.

Gordon Crum

The Mounted Riflemen in Sinai and Palestine

The Story of New Zealand's Crusaders

BY

A. BRISCOE MOORE
LATE LIEUT. AUCKLAND MOUNTED RIFLES

Illustrated by photographs taken with the N.Z.M.R. Brigade in the field

Auckland, Christchurch, Dunedin, and Wellington, N.Z.;
Melbourne and London
WHITCOMBE AND TOMBS, LIMITED

OUR UNKNOWN SOLDIER
By ADELAIDE STREET.

He gave his blood and manhood for a dream,
   Fought, suffered and endured the worst of ills;
And now the grateful nations scarcely seem
   As kind as those bare hills.

Beneath his shabby clothes white stitches shine,
   And deep marks scored by iron hot and rude;
Yet he limps proudly, never stops to whine—
   One side, he says, is good.

One side and one strong arm are firm as steel;
   He has a tent for home, and all is well.
He cannot want a shilling or a meal
   While there are trees to fell.

This man has broken kings and changed the face
   Of a great world where countless millions thrive;
To him it renders of its niggard grace
   The right to be alive.

A brother in a distant Abbey sleeps,
   Nameless and honoured, with the mighty dead;
He, far more deeply buried, lives, and keeps
   The pride to earn his bread.

All dreams are gone of home and child and wife;
   In one great cause he gave the hopes of youth.
Write this above the grave of his dead life:
   "Living, he died for Truth."

PREFACE.

This book is an attempt to do justice to the Mounted Riflemen.

The aim of the writer, whilst giving a connected account of the Campaign, is chiefly to picture to the reader the daily life and surroundings of our men in Sinai and Palestine. In doing this it is hoped to record some of the work done, about which no line has hitherto appeared in print, but which was so necessary, and so exacting on the men who performed it with such unflagging zeal.

The ceaseless patrol and outpost work in the Sinai Desert, when week after week our Mounted mens' work would be covered by the cryptic official communiqué "Nothing of importance has occurred," prompts one to draw an analogy between their doings and those of the "silent service." For it was hard and perilous work, unknown and unreported to the outside world—only fully understood by those who have taken part in it.

A description of those times will be given, and also one or two accounts of engagements reported previously in perhaps a couple of lines. Mention will be made of the country and places of historical interest through which our men passed, in an enendeavour to reveal them to the reader as these modern Crusaders saw them.

This book is not intended to be a military history. A connected story of the Campaign has been given, but the primary object has been a description of things as experienced by the men concerned.

The military reader may obtain full technical details of the various engagements from the official publication dealing with the subject. Much that has been dealt with herein is of more human than official interest.

If the aim outlined is achieved, and the reader comes to believe that the Mounted men have done their full share in worthily upholding the name of New Zealand; that their record in endurance and performance is as high as that of any British troops who fought in the Great War, then the writer will be proud to feel that he has helped towards a realization and recognition of the Mounted Riflemen's work by the people of New Zealand.

And to those who will never return to their own beautiful country, but laid down their lives in the wastes of Sinai, Palestine, and the Jordan, in the performance of this work, New Zealand surely owes her grateful appreciation; for they were gallant gentlemen who gave their lives willingly towards its completion for the good of mankind.

The Author's thanks are due to Col. Findlay for revision of the manuscript, and to Sergt. J. C. Muir and others for valuable help in compilation; also to Capt. A. Rhodes, Sergt. D'A. Lange, and Corpl. Alexander for contributions to the illustrations, and to H. N. O. Brown for permission to include the poem "Gundagai."

A. B. M.

Dunedin,
15th January, 1920.

INTRODUCTORY NOTE BY COL. FINDLAY, C.B., D.S.O., C.O. CANTERBURY MOUNTED RIFLES.

The work of our Mounted Brigade in Egypt and Palestine has throughout the War been little heard of in New Zealand, probably owing to the bigger operations in France and Flanders. That is to some extent excusable on account of the comparatively few men in a Mounted Brigade compared with an Infantry Division. The Author describes very capably the interesting and historical country operated in, and the many difficulties and hardships experienced in our various engagements. The reader should get a good general idea of the very strenuous life of a Mounted Rifleman on active service, and will have his mind disabused of the fairly common fallacy that our Mounted men were merely tourists.

JOHN FINDLAY.

CONTENTS.

CHAPTER I.
General outline of Campaign — Forces engaged — Stages — Extension of front—New Zealand Forces on front   11

CHAPTER II.
Serapeum—Suez Canal defences—The Desert—Bir Et Malar —Patrol work—Starving Bedouins—The water ration —Night Marches   18

CHAPTER III.
The fighting in August, 1916 — Advance of the Turks— Romani—Katia—Oghratina—Bir El Abd—Results   29

CHAPTER IV.
Salmana to Mustagidda—The incident of the goats—Outposts—An incident—"Standing to"—The road used by Joseph and Mary—The features of the Desert—Wire roads — Bombing — Superiority of Turks — The lighter side   34

CHAPTER V.
The horses—Care taken by men—Remounts—Comparisons— Load carried   44

CHAPTER VI.
Desert tactics—March on El Arish—Battle of Magh Daba— Christmas in the Desert—Incidents round a supply dump —Railway construction   49

CHAPTER VII.
The Rafa fight—Opinion of a German officer—Redoubt taken by New Zealand Brigade—Experiences of the wounded —A good shot—The Bedouins   57

CHAPTER VIII.
First attack on Gaza—Colonial resource—Mistaken press reports—The town of Gaza—Preparations—The second attack—Fara—Patrol encounters—Description of a troop —Railway demolition—Arrival of the donkeys   ..   65

CHAPTER IX.
How a Mounted Rifles bivouac was laid out—Life in bivouac —On trek   76

8 CONTENTS

CHAPTER X.

Advance on Beersheba—The march—The Saba fight—Fighting at Ras El Nagb—Endurance of the horses without water — A seventy mile trek — The battle of Ayun Kara 83

CHAPTER XI.

Occupation of Jaffa by New Zealand Brigade—The town—Engagements at Khirbet Hadra and Sheikh Muanis—What happened at the wine-press—Holding the trenches—Bivouacs at Sukerier and Richon Le Zion .. 94

CHAPTER XII.

Trek to the right flank—The Hills of Judea—Bethlehem—Nebi Musa—Occupation of Jericho—Description of town—First crossing of the Jordan—The Jordan Valley and River 100

CHAPTER XIII.

First attack on Amman — Objectives — The Mountains of Gilead—The Hedjaz railway—Circassians in Ain Es Sir—The Arabs—A charge by Arab horsemen—An attack by the Camel Corps—Weather conditions—Difficulties of supplies—A night attack by New Zealanders—Experiences of a signaller—Enemy shell-fire—The wounded—Withdrawal—Treachery at Ain Es Sir—Press reports—A criticism 105

CHAPTER XIV.

Bivouac near Jericho—A bombing raid—The Dead Sea—Life in the Valley—Adventures of a troop on post .. 116

CHAPTER XV.

Second Amman "stunt"—Objectives—A spell near Bethlehem—Solomon's Pools—Native methods in agriculture—Ploughing—Harvesting—Treading the corn—Winnowing—Bethlehem 125

CHAPTER XVI.

Jerusalem as the New Zealanders saw it — Situation — The Holy City—Condition after capture—Protection of holy places by British—The Holy Sepulchre—Calvary—Via Dolorosa—Jews' wailing place—Mosques of Omar and El Aksa—Vally of Jehosophat—Garden of Gethsemane — Mount of Olives — Bethany — The people of Jerusalem 130

CHAPTER XVII.

The Jordan — Enemy attack at Ain Ed Duc — Evils of the Valley in summer—Ravages of malaria—How a man was evacuated to hospital—Aotea Home—Training camp—His return to the line—"Jericho Jane" .. 141

CHAPTER XVIII.

Final operations in Palestine—Ruses employed by British—First advance—Action at Damieh—The capture of the bridge—The march up the Mountains of Gilead—Taking of Es Salt — More malaria — Advance on Amman — Cutting of Hedjaz railway—A night "stunt" by the Auckland Regiment 147

CHAPTER XIX.

The fight for Amman—Galloping into action—Capture of the town—Results—Amman, the Philadelphia of history—Turkish forces cut off to the south—The surrender at Ziza—Captures—Condition of Turks—The return to the coast *viâ* Jericho and Jerusalem—Victorious conclusion of Campaign—Casualties 162

CHAPTER XX.

After the Armistice — The Surafend incident — Canterbury leaves for Gallipoli — Rafa — Good-bye to the horses — The Egyptian Rebellion — The New Zealanders' part — Departure for New Zealand 169

LIST OF ILLUSTRATIONS.

	PAGE
Captured Officers near Amman	*Frontispiece*
A Camel Train in the Desert	16
Making a "Water Dump" in the Desert	16
Natives of Egyptian Labour Corps	17
The Desert Railway	17
A Typical Troop of Mounted Riflemen	32
Remains of an Enemy Aeroplane	33
A Good Burst	33
Map of Northern Sinai	40
A Palestine Native	48
Loading Wounded into a Hospital Train	48
A Halt during Operations	49
Gas Training	49
"Standing To" in a Wady	64
Turkish Officers Captured	65
Austrian Troops Evacuating Jerusalem	80
The N.Z.M.R. Taking Possession of Jaffa	81
A Bivouac in the Jordan Valley	96
Arabs in the Employ of the British Intelligence	96
New Zealanders Crossing the Jordan	97
A Typical East of Jordan Cut-throat	112
Jerusalem from the Mount of Olives	112
The Monastery in the Face of the Mount of Temptation	113
A Leave Party approaching the Mosque of Omar	113
Map of Southern Palestine	120
Germans Captured in the Jordan	128
New Zealanders Descending to the Jordan at Damieh	129
New Zealanders passing through Es Salt	129
Sectional Sketch illustrating Topography of Palestine Front	136
Victors and Vanquished	144
Turkish Prisoners at Amman	145
A Group of Arab Sheikhs	160
Leaving the Jordan Valley	161
New Zealanders Making Arrests in the Nile Delta	161

The Mounted Riflemen in Sinai and Palestine

CHAPTER I.

To give the reader some general idea as to the circumstances in which the New Zealand Mounted Rifles did their work, a few remarks relative to the Sinai and Palestine Campaigns will be in place.

The reader will note that the account contained in this book appertains only to the doings of the New Zealand Mounted Rifles in this double campaign, which was not their first. The Mounted Rifles had suffered severely on Gallipoli, and had returned to Egypt after the time of the evacuation in December, 1915. They went into camp at Zeitoun, near Cairo, from which place they moved out to oppose the Turks in the Sinai Desert.

In April, 1916, all the other New Zealand troops which had been in Egypt since the evacuation of Gallipoli left for France. The Mounted Rifles were then the only New Zealand troops remaining on this front.

The Egyptian Expeditionary Force, of which they formed part, was in those days a comparatively small force. At Romani, where occurred the first big Desert action, the troops engaged were the Anzac Mounted Division, a Yeomanry Brigade, and a force of infantry. The number of men concerned in the fighting did not total much over 20,000, and this was the major part of the force on this front. As the campaign progressed, this force gradually grew in numbers, notably before Gaza, where the Turks offered such a stubborn defence and held up the British for so long. At the time of the operations culminating in the Armistice with Turkey, the British force had grown from its small nucleus into an army second in numbers only to that in France. Official figures are not available at the time of writing, but, with line of communication troops, this army was numbered in hundreds of thousands.

The New Zealand Mounted Rifle Brigade was one of the very few units which took an active part in the campaign from its inception in 1915 to its close at the end of 1918. The New Zealand Brigade was essentially a fighting unit from start to finish, — a unit which suffered its full share of battle casualties, with, in the later stages of the campaign, a big proportion of loss from tropical disease. It may be said that during the whole of the campaign the Brigade took part in every major operation east of the Suez Canal — a record probably possessed by them alone.

Towards the end, when troops were so badly needed in France, some of the white divisions were withdrawn from Palestine, their places being filled by Indian troops. Some of these were Indian Cavalry, but the bulk of the mounted troops were, throughout, Australasian horsemen. In the final operations under General Allenby, probably the largest force of cavalry that has ever moved together in a concerted operation in the world's history was assembled on this front.

* * * * *

The campaign, which opened with the Turkish attempt on the Suez Canal in 1915, and ended in their utter defeat at the end of 1918, can be divided into several stages.

The first commenced with the repulse of the enemy forces which attacked the Canal. It continued through the subsequent defence of the Canal and the gradual pushing back of the Turks in the Desert; and it may be said to have ended with the fall of Magh Daba and Rafa, the two important southern outposts of the Turks on the border of Palestine.

The next stage was the clearing of the country to the Gaza-Beersheba line in southern Palestine, and the two unsuccessful attempts to take the Turkish stronghold of Gaza which resulted in such heavy loss to the British.

Up till the time of the first attack on Gaza, the campaign had been a series of actions against strongly defended enemy positions, each further forward than the last. After the first failure at Gaza, an extension of the front to the right took place. The second attack was thus on a line held by the Turks from Gaza, on the coast, to Beersheba, thirty miles inland. As the campaign progressed, so the front extended bit by bit—first to Jerusalem—then to Jericho and the Jordan. Finally, the British were operating on a front extending from the Mediterranean coast to the Hedjaz railway, east of the Jordan on the plateau beyond the mountains of Gilead. The distance across this front was 75 miles by air, but nearly 120 miles by road.

After the two unsuccessful attempts to take Gaza, came General Allenby's move in October, 1917, which turned the enemy's flank at Beersheba, and broke through the line at Gaza and elsewhere. This move was a continuation of successes which only ended when the British line lay beyond Jaffa, Jerusalem, and Jericho.

The final stage, which developed into a Turkish rout, commenced in September, 1918. A breach was made in the enemy line at an unexpected spot, through which were poured thousands of fast-moving mounted troops. These disorganised the enemy's lines of communication and finally cut them, the British mounted forces which reached Damascus and other northern points taking thousands of prisoners. On the right flank, at the same time, a force cut the Turkish line of retreat across the Jordan, and, pushing into the mountains of Gilead, seized Amman, the enemy supply depôt on the Hedjaz railway. There they secured as prisoners the garrison of the town and many Turkish troops cut off lower down the line and unable to retreat.

This advance ended in the complete defeat of the Turks, forcing them to sue for an armistice.

*　　*　　*　　*　　*

Throughout the Sinai and Palestine campaigns, the New Zealand Mounted Rifle Brigade had no official correspondent to chronicle its doings, with the result that but few people not immediately concerned have any idea of the experiences and adventures of this, for a time, almost forgotten unit. The Brigade got little official recognition from Imperial or Australian correspondents—many times, indeed, the work done by the New Zealanders was credited to others, and as the Brigade possessed no official news representative, to contradict or elucidate such reports, they usually remained unchallenged.

Although a knowledge of their accomplishments was denied to the outside world owing to the circumstances mentioned above, it may be said that amongst troops with whom they worked, our men gained and held the high reputation as first-class fighting men, on this front, that the New Zealand Division so proudly possessed in France.

New Zealand's representation in the field throughout this campaign, with but slight variation, was comprised as follows:—A Brigade of Mounted Rifles, consisting of Headquarters, Auckland, Canterbury, and Wellington Regiments; one Machine-gun squadron, one Mounted Field Ambulance; a field troop of Engineers, one Signal troop, and a mobile Veterinary Section. The strength of the New Zealand Brigade was approximately 1,850 men and 2,200 horses, although the unit was often much below this strength in the field as regards men. The New Zealand unit formed, together with the 1st, 2nd, and 3rd Australian Light Horse Brigades, the Anzac Mounted Division, although later in the campaign, after the capture of Rafa, the 3rd Light Horse were detached to make up another Division.

In addition to the above troops, New Zealand maintained a company of New Zealand Army Service Corps, employed in the Divisional Train, and two companies of Camel Corps. Towards the end of the Campaign, when the Imperial Camel Corps was disbanded, the two New Zealand companies were formed into a second New Zealand Machine-gun Squadron, which, however, was not attached to the New Zealand Brigade, but did excellent service with an Australian unit in another division. There was also, in Palestine, a force of several hundred Rarotongans. These Islanders were employed on the lines of communication, and did yeoman service in unloading stores landed on the coast in surf boats, and in handling

A camel train in the desert.

Making a "water dump" in the desert. In the foreground are seen the 15-gallon "fanatis" in which the water was carried on camels.

Natives of the Egyptian Labour Corps on railway construction in the desert.

The Desert Railway.

heavy shells in ammunition dumps. They gained the reputation of being the smartest and strongest body of men on this work on the whole front.

The base training camp, through which passed all reinforcements for the Brigade arriving from New Zealand, and men returning to duty from hospital, was situated at Moascar. This was on the fringe of the Desert, near the Suez Canal town of Ismailia, on the railway which runs from Port Said to Suez. During 1918, this camp was moved to a new and better locality on the shore of Lake Timsah, one of the canal lakes. This was a much more congenial spot and gave the opportunity of plenty of healthy bathing in the intervals of training.

In this camp all newly arrived reinforcements received their final training before being sent up the line to replace casualties. This training consisted chiefly of the use of gas-masks, musketry, and field work. Sufficient horses were kept to mount a squadron at a time, and were constantly employed in mounted training.

A training cadre of officers and non-commissioned officers was maintained, these instructors being detailed from regiments in the field for a tour of duty extending over three months.

Chapter II.

After the return to Egypt from Gallipoli, the Brigade was for some time encamped at Zeitoun, about seven miles out of Cairo.

In January, 1916, the Mounted Rifles marched out from this camp, and, heading to the east, left the verdure of the Nile Delta for the sand of Serapeum. There they bivouacked on the west bank of the Suez Canal not far from the Great Bitter Lake. Much training was done in field work in the different formations for moving across the desert that were shortly to be employed on the Sinai Peninsula. Towards the end of the stay there one squadron at a time was sent over the Canal to do patrol duty, in front of the British defences protecting this vital waterway. At the end of February the Brigade crossed the Canal, and for some time occupied a section of these defences, perhaps ten miles in length, out in the desert ten or twelve miles from the Canal. The positions were entrenched, and our men had an endless task shovelling sand, which drifted into the trenches almost as fast as they could take it out. At the same time they were called on to do long patrols out into the Desert, feeling for any move of the Turks which might be threatening the Suez Canal. It was while holding these positions, protecting the waterway of so much importance to the Empire, that the New Zealand Mounted Brigade received its first and only visit from the Prince of Wales.

The time spent in those parts was dreary and monotonous for all concerned, and is fairly well reflected in the following lines of a soldier poet who was moved to this expression of his feelings at the time:—

> Twenty miles from nowhere,
> Where the sun is hot as 'ell,
> And a breeze was never heard of—
> The Mounteds knew it well.
>
> In a sandy blisterin' 'ollow,
> 'Neath a hazy azure sky,
> Lay the sun-browned cussin' Mounteds
> At a post called Gundagai.
>
> There were trenches all around 'em,
> There was tanglefoot there, too,
> There was damn all blinkin' water,
> But heaps of bully stew.
>
> Of drinks there never was none,
> And coves you'd 'ear 'em sigh,
> If you talked of nights at Zeitoun,
> 'Fore they left for Gundagai.
>
> Of a wash they've most forgotten,
> Or of brushin' boots or 'air,
> But them don't count for nothin'
> Twenty miles from out nowhere.

For there ain't no blanky tram-cars,
  Nor pretty girls' glad eye—
No week-end dancing parties
  Way out at Gundagai.

Yet they mostly all are happy,
  Tho' one was heard to cry,
"Gott strafe the cove wot chased us
  To this bleedin' Gundagai."

And our horses, too, are thinking
  That this summer's turned to drought,
As they come in from patrolling,
  With their tongues all hangin' out.

While the 'skeeters 'um around 'em,
  And the cruel camel fly
Makes 'em wish they 'adn't 'listed,
  Since they've come to Gundagai.

But the boys have just been cheerin'
  For the news it just 'as come,
That the Abduls is approachin'
  But they'll soon be on the run.

The wait's been long and weary,
  But at last they're comin' nigh,
And they've many scores to settle,
  Have the lads at Gundagai.

Yes, they've many scores to settle,
  Mostly things from Anzac's shore,
Where there's not a cove amongst 'em,
  Didn't leave one pal or more.

But they've sworn that they'll avenge 'em,
  And each man's prepared to die,
For the reckoning of his cobbers,
  In a go at Gundagai.

Fate decreed, however, that our men were not to meet the Turks in battle in this part of the Desert, but they were not to have long to wait.

Leaving the sandy trenches and the barren wastes which had been scoured by so many patrols, on the first of April, Serapeum was reached the same day. Then, in a few days, the Brigade trekked through to Salhieh, an unsalubrious spot west of Kantara.

During this march the mounted men stopped one night in the sand at Moascar, where "Goodbyes" were said to the last of the New Zealand Infantry leaving for France, many brave fellows parting to meet no more in this world.

Arrived at Salhieh, training continued, to be rudely interrupted on one occasion in a most unpleasant manner by a full-sized sandstorm of true desert fury, which smothered everyone and everything while it lasted. From Salhieh the Brigade moved one evening in intense anticipation at an hour's notice, and marching all night reached Kantara early next morning. This sudden move was on account of a raid by the Turks on Oghratina, Katia, and Duidar, where they had surrounded and cut up the yeomanry at the first two places named, and penetrated to within about 12 miles of the Canal.

The Turks had withdrawn precipitately again out of reach, after their raid; consequently the New Zealanders were halted at Hill 70, about seven miles east of the Suez Canal at Kantara.

There training continued, but the Brigade on one occasion marched out to Romani in support of an Australian Brigade on reconnaissance, the route followed being through very loose, deep sand, a distance of about 20 miles.

It was on this, their first "Brigade stunt" right out into the wastes of the Sinai Desert, that the New Zealanders got their first real experience of what thirst could be. At this time it was the practice to ride twenty minutes, walk ten minutes, ride twenty minutes, and spell for ten minutes in every hour of a march. This practice was later discontinued, as it was found to be too wearing on the men, while the constant mounting and dismounting with a fully loaded saddle also affected the horses.

On the day of the march in question, the sun flamed from a brazen sky, and the heavy walking through the shifting sand, in the intense heat, leading an often dragging horse, gave the men a maddening thirst. It was a killing march, but, as always, a few cheerful spirits could not be suppressed. One of these was heard to remark to his neighbour, a boy nearly exhausted by the long march after a night on horsepicket—"Don't open your mouth so wide, Bill, when you yawn—you'll be getting your stummick sunburnt, an' it hurts somethin' awful!"

Romani was reached about four in the afternoon, but water was not available till late in the evening, when it was eagerly gulped down parched throats.

The Brigade returned to Hill 70, where they remained about a month, training continuing the whole time. Then came a move to Bir Et Malar, farther out in the Desert, where May found them bivouacked. Here they were to remain till August, with the exception of a brief spell at Kantara, before being called on to take part in the historic fighting at Romani. When the Brigade moved back for this short spell, Wellington Regiment remained out in the Desert, being attached to the 2nd Brigade of Australian Light Horse, with which they worked till after the fighting in August. Their place in the New Zealand Brigade was temporarily taken by an Australian Regiment.

When our men first moved out to Bir Et Malar, they experienced the greatest difficulty in getting their horses to drink the brackish desert water. The horses afterwards became more or less accustomed to it, but did not drink it freely. During the stay there, a patrol one day found an old Bedouin and three children in a palm tree "hod" away out in the Desert. The old man was squatting on his haunches before a pile of camel dung, busily engaged in picking out what undigested grain he could find. This and a few dry dates apparently formed their sole means of subsistence, which was barely keeping life in their poor starved bodies. The men of the patrol put the old fellow on a horse, and carrying the youngsters before them on their saddles, took them into the bivouac.

There they were fed and photographed, before being sent down to the Base, where, no doubt, they lived in greater luxury than they had ever known before. Such Bedouins were occasionally encountered, nearly always in a state of starvation.

From the bivouac at Bir Et Malar the New Zealanders were constantly called out on patrol and reconnaissance work of the most trying kind, commonly being summoned at half an hour's notice to take part in a "stunt" of from one to four days in length. It was important work, made necessary by the continual menace of Turkish aggression towards the Canal which lay behind our forces.

In those days most of the men were still comparatively "new at the game," and turning out at such short notice in full marching order with all necessary supplies taxed them severely. A man had to draw his own rations, fill his waterbottle, and draw his horse's rations. This last had to be done up in nosebags and secured properly to the saddle, this being no mean art in itself. Horses had to be saddled, picket and head-ropes done up, and all necessary gear strapped to saddles. Besides these main items there was a host of minor details to be attended to incidental to turning out fully equipped for what the adventure might bring forth.

Later in the campaign, when men became expert in this sort of thing, half an hour's notice would be ample, and the appointed time for moving would find every man ready without any apparent rush. Any stragglers would usually be found to be new men not thoroughly practised in the art of turning out and perhaps deceived by the unhurrying haste of their comrades with more experience.

The water ration was most precious, this consisting of but one waterbottle per man per day. This was the sole issue of fresh water, which could only be supplemented for ablution purposes at times by a trickle of the bitter brackish desert water, often collected most laboriously over long hours in jam tins or other small receptacles.

In the great heat of the blazing desert the temptation to drink freely was well-nigh irresistible, but every man had to exercise the greatest care, and no more than sip at his water-bottle. Water supplies were uncertain, no one knowing definitely how long it would be before more was available on these desert adventures.

It was usual to leave the bivouac at Bir Et Malar in the evening and march all night, the heat being too intense for much movement by day, unless it was absolutely necessary. During the fierce heat of the day the force on patrol would, when possible, seek the shade of some feathery date palms, which offered sanctuary in scattered "hods" far apart in the endless rolling hills and hollows of the Sinai Desert.

During the night heavy fogs would often

complicate the already difficult travelling in the dark without landmarks, and daylight, on one occasion at least, found the advance guard on the tail of their own rear guard, the force during the night having travelled in a circle but a few miles from the starting point. On these night marches it was a common occurrence for a man to fall asleep in his saddle. With head sunk on chest and body moving automatically with his horse, he would be carried on by his faithful plodding steed. A man would ride for long distances like this, only waking up when his horse wandered from his companions, and, passing the troop-leader, collided with the troop in front. Then would the sleeper dazedly pull himself together, thicken the air with a few choice imprecations, and resume his original place in the column, often to repeat the performance again during the night. A column sent out like this on reconnaissance was dependent on camel trains for supplies, these usually coming up in the evening with water, horse fodder, and rations. The water was carried in fifteen gallon fanatis, or as they were more commonly called, "fantasies," and was often almost too hot to drink, after travelling for hours in these metal tanks exposed to the sun — not the best kind of thirst-quenchers for parched throats, but eagerly drunk by the thirsty horsemen for all that.

On the 16th of May the Canterbury Regiment had an unenviable experience whilst engaged on work of this kind. Going out on reconnaissance to Debabis, a spot where water was supposed to be available, they found that the Turks had been there before them, and no water was to be had. The Regiment had to journey back to Oghratina in the heat of the day, from which place word was sent in for the camel trains. Ninety men were struck down with sunstroke, the heat being 118° in the shade.

At one spot, where the New Zealanders had frequently to water, there were one or two disused wells of very brackish water, which could be bucketed up, and there could be seen horse and rider drinking the filthy stuff side by side out of the same trough, the water often making the men very sick afterwards.

Throughout this period the heat was almost unendurable, and flies, mosquitoes, and midges contributed their quota to the already sufficient hardships of the life. People at home, who have never experienced the flies of Egypt, cannot realize what a persistent and exasperating curse they can be, clustering in black clouds over everything, hardly deigning to leave the food one is eating even as it is swallowed. The horses were provided with cord fly-fringes which were attached to the browbands of their head-collars, and the men were supplied with a number of fly whisks for "swatting" the insects, but these did little to minimise the evil.

The men's rations were often indifferent, consisting largely of "bully" beef and "hard tack." Many men were afflicted with a form of sand colic, which made it almost impossible for them to eat during the heat of the day without immediately vomiting. As the New Zealanders became experienced in the desert life, it became the custom to eat and drink little except in the cool of the evening and early morning —this was particularly so as regards drinking. Thus did the New Zealand horsemen live while guarding the frontiers of Empire in the wide spaces of the Desert of Sinai.

While at Bir Et Malar an incident occurred not without its humorous side. The Brigade got sudden notice one evening to "stand-to" as the result of a message announcing the approach of a cyclone in their direction. For hours, late into the night, all hands were on the alert, horses saddled and everything ready for an immediate move. It then transpired that the message had been mangled in transmission, and really related to a consignment of "cyclone wire" which was being forwarded for use in some defensive works!

Chapter III.

On the 29th of May the New Zealanders left Bir Et Malar for Salmana. The following day was spent keeping out of sight in some palm trees at Debabis. Moving on at night, they arrived at Salmana early the following morning, where they had their first action of any consequence against the Turks on this front. It was, however, only a very brief affair, although aeroplanes did a good deal of damage to the retiring enemy. Returning to bivouac that night, our men experienced their first bombing raid the next morning, the forerunner of many to come, when the enemy's bombs caused heavy casualties in both horses and men of an Australian Brigade adjoining the New Zealanders.

Towards the beginning of August, a force of Turks, estimated at about eighteen thousand in number, advanced towards our positions; a somewhat remarkable achievement over roughly a hundred miles of desert, carrying water, rations, machine-guns and ammunition, and dragging one heavy 6 inch gun in addition to field guns. Some idea of the difficulties of moving field guns, let alone a heavy gun such as this, may be had when it is mentioned that it took a team of 24 horses to drag a British

4·5 Howitzer through the heavy sand. The endurance of the Turkish infantry must have been extraordinary to have covered this distance over the yielding surface of the desert. The supply of water was always a problem, as our men knew to their cost, always involving a long string of slow moving camel transport for its carriage from the very few sources of supply.

The Turks moved on Romani on the night of the 3rd of August, and delivered their attack against the British positions in a strong attempt to turn our flank and cut the communications of our desert force in the rear. The action developed in the darkness of the early morning hours against the Australians on this flank, who throughout the day fought a sanguinary combat against heavy odds. They were reinforced during the day by infantry, and then a force composed of the New Zealand Brigade and a Brigade of Yeomanry, supported by Infantry, descended on the exposed left flank of the Turks with crushing force. This turned the tide of battle, and a general attack at dawn the next day completed the demoralization of the enemy, who withdrew to reform his broken scattered line at Katia. The New Zealanders played a big part in these operations, at the cost of many good men. Several thousand Turks were taken prisoner, and much material was captured.

Here should be mentioned the work done by the Wellington Regiment and the two Australian Regiments with which they were brigaded. These units were constantly in touch with the Turks night and day for about a fortnight before the Romani fight, as the enemy moved forward in the Desert, men and guns reinforcing him constantly from El Arish.

The work was most trying, as our men continually came under fire without the chance of hitting back, all the while sustaining casualties. On the night of the Turkish advance an isolated post of our men some miles out in the desert was cut off and surrounded between the two enemy columns. One man only got out, which he did by taking a very bold course. Riding alongside one of the Turkish columns in the dark, he waited his chance until an opening in the column presented itself, when he made his way through without being recognised, and so back to the British lines as fast as his horse could carry him through the heavy sand.

Following up the retreating Turks as fast as their weary horses could move, the New Zealanders came into collision with them again at Katia, six miles further on in the Desert. There our men made a frontal attack on the Turkish positions, which was strongly resisted by the enemy. The action, however, was doomed to be indecisive, for the Turks withdrew at night.

In this fight a unique spectacle was witnessed which is worth mention. The 5th Australian Light Horse, Canterbury and Auckland rode into action in swift moving waves. The Australian Regiment galloped in with bayonets fixed and dismounted for action—an inspiring sight as these splendid horsemen moved over the sand into battle with their steel-tipped rifles flashing in the sun. This was, perhaps, the first time that a mounted unit not armed with swords had carried the naked steel into action this way on their chargers.

On the 7th of August the Brigade made a demonstration against the Turks at Oghratina, when the enemy once more withdrew under cover of darkness. The following day the New Zealanders pushed on to Debabis, and early in the morning of the 9th August came into action against the Turks at Bir El Abd, driving them back three or four miles. During the day the enemy was heavily reinforced, and thus enabled to put up a stiff resistance which accounted for many more casualties amongst our men. Shortage of water compelled the withdrawal of the New Zealand Brigade that night, when they moved back to Oghratina, but on the 12th they again advanced and occupied Bir El Abd, from which the Turks had meantime withdrawn. On the taking of Oghratina, our men found that the Turks had left a very elaborate trench system. They also found a note left by the enemy, stating that they had captured one New Zealand officer and seven men. This was the post that had been surrounded out in the Desert from Romani. The missive warningly concluded that if the New Zealanders followed the Turks

A typical Troop of Mounted Riflemen.

Shot down. Remains of an enemy aeroplane. Note German cross just visible on tail.

A good burst.

too far into the Desert it would be at their own risk, and their blood would be upon their own heads.

In this August fighting the Turkish force which had moved across the Desert to Romani with the confident anticipation of wiping the British off the map had been badly mauled. Approximately 9,000 Turks were made prisoners — half their total force — and after the fighting at Bir El Abd the shattered remnant withdrew for reorganisation to El Arish, 50 miles away on the coast.

It should be mentioned that after the fighting at Romani practically all the work fell on the horsemen of the Anzac Mounted Division, the heavy going in the deep Desert sand precluding any rapid movement of dismounted troops.

Chapter IV.

Strenuous patrol and outpost work was then once again the lot of the New Zealanders, most of it directed to covering the advance of the railway, which was being pushed on as rapidly as possible across the Desert in rear of the troops. This continued through Salmana, Kasseiba, Mossefig, Mazar, and Mustagidda, from which last-named place the advance on El Arish was launched. A bivouac was established at each place named, which formed a base for the troops employed in the surrounding country, as they moved forward step by step, continually feeling and watching for any sudden descent of the enemy, who had proved he was no mean adversary in the Desert.

Little was heard of the mounted men during this time, the tale of patrols and outposts being unsung and almost unrecorded, but it was a stern duty to the men concerned.

Patrols often meant constant hard riding in superheated saddles, over mile after mile of burning, yielding sand, with every man continually on the alert, as the little force, usually a troop in strength, travelled in open formation across the Desert with no other guide than the flickering prismatic compass carried by the leader. By night, movement would be made in somewhat closer formation, direction being kept by the stars and the luminous marks on the compass, combined with the native sense of direction of the leader.

In such featureless country, where one mound was like a thousand others, and detours had often to be made round high sand ridges, the greatest skill and accuracy were necessary to reach the desired points. Inattention or carelessness would mean the loss of direction, when many hours might be taken up before the true course to the objective was found once again. It was in this work that our men, used to wide open spaces and reliance upon their own initiative, always excelled.

The nights on outpost were long hours of watchfulness, with the horses screened by a ridge or hidden in a hollow. Few were the hours of sleep, as each man took his turn on sentry or on horse-picket, the horses requiring constant attention. In the morning, usually about 3 a.m., before dawn, every man would be called to "stand to."

This "standing to" every morning was a feature of the Desert campaign which always shortened the hours of sleep. All hands would have to turn out dressed, saddle the horses, tie horsefeed and other necessary gear to their saddles, and be ready to move at a moment's notice, this being the most likely hour in the twenty-four for the enemy to attempt a descent on our men from the shadowy hollows and dim spaces of the Desert in front of the outpost line. Such nights on outpost were not unrelieved by occasional humorous incidents. One night a troop-leader, having disposed his troop on post, and given strict instructions to the first sentry to call him at once should *anything* approach the post, rolled himself up in his canvas "flea-bag" for a sleep.

It happened that this particular sentry was a man who fancied he had an old score against his troop-leader to pay off. Consequently, when he observed a desert jackal padding over the sand towards him, he saw his opportunity. He sent one of his mates to arouse the sleeping officer with the warning—"Something is moving over the desert towards us." It should be mentioned that this officer had not been long with the Brigade, and was not very experienced in night work. Alarmed by the warning, which, doubtless, conveyed a picture to his imaginative mind of swarms of Turks descending upon him, he scrambled out of his sleeping-bag. In his haste, however, one spur caught in the canvas, and he turned a somersault, while his ready cocked revolver went off with a bang and a flash in the darkness. The report alarmed the rest of the force on outpost, who immediately thought there must be "something doing," and got ready for anything to happen. It was subsequently hard for the principal actor in the little comedy to explain what caused all the commotion. He was for a time distinctly unpopular. The only man thoroughly satisfied was the sentry.

The monotony of the life was unvaried, leave at this time being almost unknown, and not granted to the men of the Brigade until much later, when they were practically out of the Desert, and one cannot but admire the faithfulness and efficiency with which they carried out their thankless task in these times. Even when in bivouac the Mounted Riflemen had plenty to do, with the minimum of comfort. While at Bir Et Malar tents were provided for the men, but in the heat of the day they often preferred to find shelter in the shade of a palm tree, so hot did they become. Throughout the rest of the Desert Campaign, the soldier's shelter consisted merely of a blanket or two stretched over a couple of palm leaf sticks. The often uninviting rations could seldom be supplemented with canteen supplies, so great was the congestion on the single line of railway caused by absolutely necessary supplies of material alone. At Kasseiba a herd of some thirty or forty goats was rounded up and brought into bivouac by a patrol, which had found them wandering on the Desert. Knives were sharpened in joyful preparation, many anticipating a change from the usual "bully" to a meal of fresh meat. Unfortunately, these happy anticipations were not justified — All the animals proved to be veterans, and the opinion was freely expressed that they were direct descendants of the pair from the Ark, that had been wandering in those parts since their liberation on Mt. Ararat.

Mention should be made here of the good work done by the Pioneers. These Field Engineers were constantly out in small parties ahead of the other troops, finding and constructing watering places ready for the next move forward—often in the course of this work isolated miles out in the Desert, where any enterprising party of Turks could have cut them off. It is interesting to record, that, in their passages across the Sinai Desert, the New Zealanders traversed the ancient caravan route between Egypt and Palestine, over which in Biblical times Joseph and Mary travelled with the infant Christ. This way was also taken by Napoleon in 1799, the New Zealand Brigade watering at Katia at Napoleon's wells.

It is difficult to give a graphic picture of this time in the Desert, so few were the features of interest outside the daily routine. Later, in Palestine, the surroundings in which our men found themselves nearly always possessed some interest. At least the landscape was varied, whereas this could not be said of the Desert. This barren waste was always the same, except when whipped to fury in a blinding sandstorm. In every direction, as far as the wearied eye could see, was sand, sand, sand, — white and glaring. For the most part the Desert was undulating, in gradual hills and hollows, broken now and then by a ridge built up by some freak of the wind, with a gradual slope on one side and a steep descent on the other. In places a dry stunted scrub broke the white glare, which was otherwise unrelieved except for the occasional clumps of date-palms, whose graceful tops just showed out of some slight hollow. These palms were most useful to our men in many ways. They offered cover from observation by enemy aeroplanes, and their grateful shade was always welcome during the day. The central ribs of their big leaves provided sticks to support blankets in the erection of a "bivvy." While last, but not least, in September and October their fruit was a healthy adjunct to army rations.

After the August fighting, a patrol scouring the Desert near the coast came suddenly upon a patch of water-melons growing in the sand. These were eagerly consumed by many, but the sudden change from the hard diet they had been used to had a disastrous effect on hardened "tummies" all round, and resulted in many bad pains under the belt!

On the commencement of the Desert Campaign, the British attempted to follow up the troops with a metalled road running roughly parallel to the railway. The difficulties of construction, however, were so great, that after a few miles this was abandoned, and an expedient was discovered in the wire road, which successfully met requirements for the passage of infantry and light wheeled vehicles. A road of this kind was laid from Kantara right through the Desert into Southern Palestine.

It consisted of four widths of ordinary wire-netting, about one and a half inch mesh, pegged down into the sand in a double layer. It was thus about twelve feet in width, and excellent to walk on after footing it through the heavy sand. It was almost an essential to the movement of infantry for any distance across the Desert.

* * * *

The enemy had made his first serious bombing raid at Romani, where his bombs did frightful damage to the men and horses of an Australian Brigade, and throughout this period he indulged in almost daily aeroplane raids, his objective generally being railhead and the precious water supplies. This incessant bombing continued until the latter part of 1917, up to which time the Turks were easily our superiors in the air, most of their pilots, however, being Germans and Austrians. It should be said that their superiority was not due to the personal element, but to the fact that they possessed much better and faster machines than the British force on this front. The New Zealanders were constant admirers of the exploits of our airmen in machines which were hopelessly outclassed by those of the enemy.

Owing largely to the scattered formation

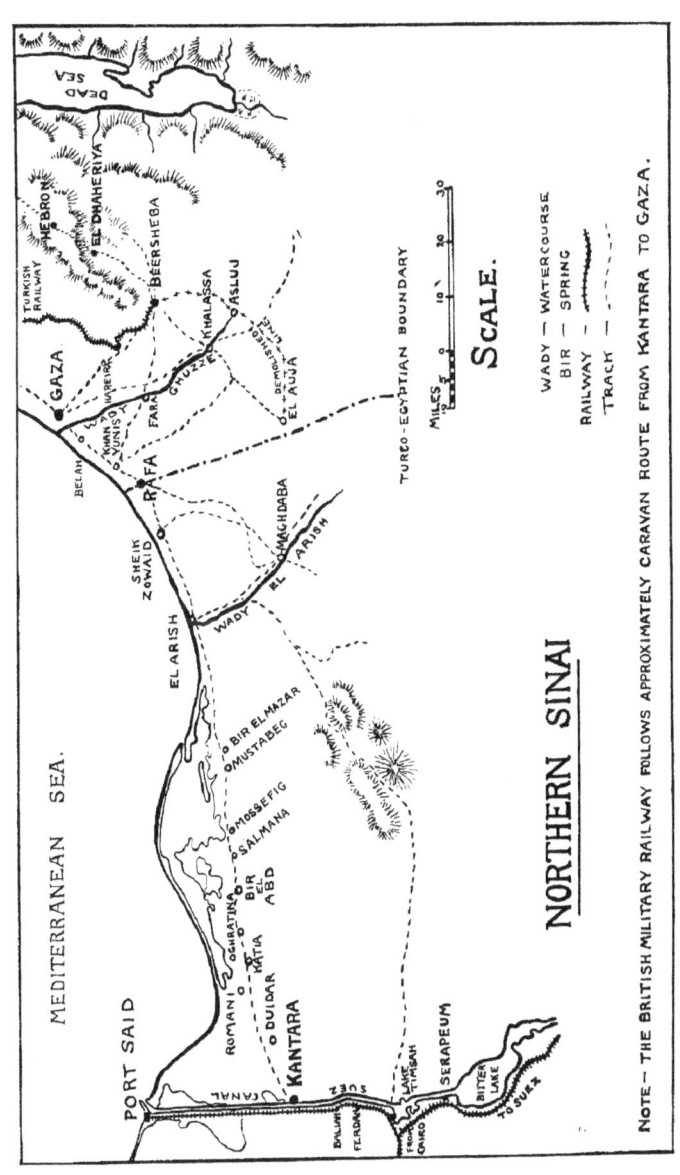

adopted by the New Zealand Brigade when in Bivouac, after the lesson learnt at Romani, where the enemy caught horses and men in close formation, their losses from bombing were not heavy. On the other hand, the continued aerial attention of the Turk at this time caused a lot of extra and very harassing work with the constant alarms involving the necessity of leading the horses off the lines on the approach of an enemy 'plane.

Added to this, of course, was the nervous strain to which all hands were subjected. For, as everyone knows who has experienced it, aerial bombing is one of the most trying episodes in a soldier's life. When an aeroplane is overhead at a high altitude intent on dropping a number of death-dealing bombs to the best advantage, everyone for a wide distance around feels that the 'plane must be directly above him. The growing hiss of a released bomb, and the deafening crash and vicious whirring that succeeds it, does not do much to allay anxiety till the marauder has completed his work and disappeared elsewhere; and the bloody mess that is the result of a good hit does not increase one's appreciation of this almost daily item in the entertainment.

The only measures of protection against aircraft, as far as our men were concerned, were machine-guns cn improvised mountings, and field guns sunk in pits to give the necessary elevation, but these were not effective in checking the expeditions of the enemy's airmen.

Trying as they were, these bombing raids were at times productive of some amusing incidents, as in the case of one of the first alarms, when a well-known character in the Brigade, noted for his dry remarks, was observed crouching behind a small mound, vindictively emptying his revolver in the direction of an aeroplane at least four thousand feet above him.

On another occasion, an equally well-known character in charge of some camels, who had formerly been a sailor, was heard, during the rush to get horses and camels off the lines, to bawl at the top of his voice, "Cut them (adjective) camels adrift fore and aft!" At this time the course followed on the sound of the aeroplane alarm was to loosen all horses from the picket line and scatter with them in every direction, so as to offer but a poor target for bombs. This system was later discontinued, partly on account of the disorganization resulting from its frequent repetition.

Another individual, given to the use of nautical terms when strongly moved, entertained those near him one day in similar fashion. One trooper, in his haste to get himself and horse well out of the way, had freed his mount's headrope, but not the heelrope, and was on the horse's back vainly digging in his heels. The horse, of course, remained tethered by one hind leg, and was somewhat bored by his master's undue hurry. At this point a voice in the rear was heard to drawl — "Go astern, man, go astern!"

At the time of the first raid at Romani, a senior officer of the New Zealand Brigade was the star turn in a truly "moving" picture that would have delighted the hearts of any audience. Some Indians of a camel train near his quarters showed signs of clearing out without proper attention to their charges, when this officer, bounding out of his bivouac in raiment of many colours, to wit, a pair of new pyjamas, leaped on to an agile Arab pony which he always rode, and with lurid language and much flourishing of a stockwhip rounded the scared natives up, and indicated to them in forceful terms their path of duty. The first bomb which landed amongst the Australians on this day stampeded many of their horses. As they came galloping through the New Zealand bivouac with manes and tails flying and nostrils distended, their fear of this new terror from the sky seemed to communicate itself to the New Zealand horses, which also would have stampeded in like fashion had our men not seen the trouble in time and rushed to their heads.

Chapter V.

At different times during the slow progression across the Desert, the horses were often short of rations, and almost continually had bad water to drink—often not enough even of that. These were added cares to the majority of the men, who had the welfare of their faithful chargers so much at heart. This individual care for their horses, indeed, was one of the outstanding characteristics of the New Zealand horsemen, and largely made possible the long marches and consistently good patrol work done by them. Men would go to all sorts of trouble to gain a little extra feed or water for their horses, and in bivouac, or on the march, do everything to save them, and preserve them in the best possible condition.

At one time the horses were badly affected by the bad water, and sand colic, and as the strength of the Brigade was measured by the men it could mount, for some time the units were very much below strength, owing to the wholesale evacuation of sick and collapsed horses. Many of the remounts sent up to replace the worn out chargers were not New Zealand horses, but came, originally, it was thought, from the Argentine. These animals, although apparently in the pink of condition when they arrived, were soft, of poor heart, and could not stand up to the hardships as the original New Zealand-bred horses had done, with the result that they were evacuated from the active list as fast as they appeared.

At this point it will be apposite to state that on this front, where in the later days of the Campaign in Palestine the New Zealanders took part in the largest cavalry movements seen in the world's history, the New Zealand horses throughout stood up to their work brilliantly, and were considered, by many qualified to express an opinion, to be, perhaps, the most serviceable troop-horses in the world for active service.

The mounts possessed by the Australians were, generally speaking, better looking horses, and were held by some to be the best horses, but veterinary returns will show that they did not stand up to hardship as did the New Zealand-bred stock.

As regards the English Yeomanry, the New Zealand horses were superior in both appearance and stamina.

The load carried by a Mounted Rifleman's horse in the field is considerable, and may be described here in some detail, to give the reader some idea of what is required of these horses in endurance. The description given is of the minimum load carried when setting out on a "stunt" (as all individual operations against the enemy came to be called), consisting of bare essentials only.

The Mounted Rifleman wore, on his person, a leather bandolier containing 150 rounds of ammunition, bayonet, service rifle, and haversack, the latter usually stuffed with tins of the inevitable "bully" beef and army biscuits. The saddlery on his mount consisted of headstall and bridle, headrope, picketing rope, saddle, and blanket. In addition to this the horse carried, slung round his neck, a leather sand muzzle, which was slipped on in place of the nosebag when he had finished his meagre feed, to prevent him eating sand and dirt; this being a bad habit quickly indulged in by many horses when hungry.

In this sand-muzzle the trooper often carried his mess-tin, or "billy" for cooking or making tea, and his dandy brush for grooming. The next item was the horse bandolier, slung round the horse's neck and containing an additional 90 rounds of ammunition. Strapped on the front of the saddle were two leather wallets, probably containing towel, soap, spare shirt, socks, and what rations the rider could not get into his haversack; strapped on top of these again would be the greatcoat and one blanket.

The men usually set out with forty-eight hours' rations and an iron ration, while the horse ration for three days (27 lbs.) would be carried. This horsefeed would be distributed between two nosebags, tied to the side of the saddle, and a sandbag, round which might be rolled a ground or bivouac sheet, strapped across the rear of the saddle. Also slung to the side of the saddle would be the canvas water-bucket which served the soldier for the watering of his horse and his own ablutions, and his water-bottle. When the Desert was behind them, and our troops were in Palestine, where a sufficiency of water was usually obtainable, two or three water-bottles would be carried by each man.

Besides the above, some men carried a spare haversack made into a saddlebag, and strapped to the side of the saddle, while at least one man in each section of four had to carry as well a sack for anchoring the picket line of his section in the sand. Another addition to the load which was often seen was a small bundle of firewood strapped to the rear of the saddle, this being often unobtainable on the march, and a necessity for the production of a New Zealander's stand-by, a "boil-up" of tea. The tunic, which was needed at night, was usually carried strapped to the top of the load, the rider wearing an armless singlet or shirt which protected his body from sunburn.

Considerable skill was required in adjusting the load described above, as an unequal distribution of weight, loose ends of straps getting underneath the saddle, or a wrinkled saddle-blanket, would quickly give a horse a sore back on the long marches the New Zealand horsemen were constantly called on to do.

From the foregoing it will easily be understood that a man of medium weight would ride, with all his gear up, at well over twenty stone, a huge weight for a light horse to carry for long distances on good going, let alone through the heavy sand of the Desert.

A pathetic sight was often to be seen during brief halts on a long march, for the faithful, tired animals would often lie down, with all their gear on, beside their wearied masters, to snatch what brief repose they could.

Loading wounded into a hospital train from camel cacolets.

A halt during operations.

Gas training. Our men passing through gas clouds with their gas helmets on.

Chapter VI.

The formation adopted by the Brigade for its own protection when moving across the Desert, liable at any time to attack by the enemy, was what is now known as the "screen" formation. This method was adopted as the result of Desert experience, and, in the wide unenclosed spaces traversed, proved most efficacious. The advance guard threw out a long screen of men riding some distance apart from each other, who moved forward as feelers on a wide front. From each flank of this moving screen the flank guards were strung out to the rear in another thin line of horsemen, the rear of the force being protected in like manner.

Some distance inside the screens moved the main body, while between it and the long line of scouts were the troops acting in support of the screen. Usually each four men in the scouting line were supported by the remainder of their troop some distance behind them. On the advanced screen of scouts being held up by enemy fire, these supporting troops would be thrown into the part of the line that was menaced with the object of breaking down the

D

opposition and allowing the main force to continue its progress without wasting valuable time in deployment. On coming into contact with a strong body of the enemy, such as in the early stages of a general engagement, the line formed by the screen and its supports would be gradually built up from the rear, as the main body deployed and came into action.

It was from Mustagidda, the last bivouac occupied in this stage of the Desert Campaign, that the New Zealand Brigade made its descent on El Arish, a spot on the coast held by the Turks, long desired by the British. At the time the Brigade moved out from the bivouac it was not known that a march on El Arish was immediately contemplated—all hands thought this was merely another step forward in the Desert to a bivouac a few miles further on. The Christmas mail from home had just been received, and as the column moved out many men resembled travelling Christmas trees, with parcels containing the good things from New Zealand tied all over themselves and horses. Many also carried long "bivvy" sticks for rigging up their next temporary blanket shelter, and these sticking up in the air enhanced the general comical effect. When it became known that the column was bound for El Arish, where fighting was expected, parcels, sticks, and all other unnecessary gear were shed right and left into the Desert, until everyone was in fighting trim. This necessitated later the telling of many "white lies" in letters home as to the enjoyment of cakes and other good things that were never eaten.

The march on El Arish, a distance of thirty-five miles through the heavy sand, was done in the one night, straight across the Desert on a compass bearing. By those knowing the Desert, and the difficulties of keeping direction, it was recognized as a fine piece of work, and a credit to the young officer who so ably led the column. Contrary to expectations, El Arish was occupied without opposition from the Turks, who had just evacuated it, this making another big step forward for the British troops in the Desert.

The New Zealand Brigade was at this time part of what was known as the Desert Column, under General Sir Philip Chetwoode; this was later, with the addition of other troops, formed into the Desert Mounted Corps, and came under the command of General Sir H. Chauvel.

Leaving El Arish on 22nd December, 1916, a bitterly cold night, the Brigade marched down the Wady El Arish, the River of Egypt of ancient history. This was the first occasion on which the horses had been on hard ground since leaving the Suez Canal. Marching all night, and covering a distance of nearly thirty miles, the New Zealanders shortly after dawn came into collision with the Turks at Magh Daba. After a stiff engagement the place fell into the hands of the Desert Column, which was thus another and important step forward in the campaign to reach the Holy Land; Magh Daba forming, with Rafa, one of the southern outposts of the Turkish Empire.

After the battle at Magh Daba the New Zealanders moved back to El Arish, where they spent Christmas and New Year in bivouac on the beach beside the Mediterranean — the weather, unfortunately, being cold and wet, it being then the middle of the rainy season.

When the Brigade moved back, one regiment was left behind on the scene of the action to clean up, bury the dead, and escort the convoys of wounded back to El Arish. Leaving Magh Daba late in the afternoon, night soon fell, and it was finally decided to camp till daylight. This was on Christmas Eve, which could have been spent in more festive places than the barren gloom of the Desert. Moving at dawn, the bivouac area was soon reached by daylight, where a very tame Christmas was experienced. The central item in the menu was good old "high explosive" army "duff," practically everyone having shed their Christmas gifts, received at Mustagidda, into the Desert on the night of the advance.

It was when our men were in a bivouac, such as that at El Arish, for a brief spell, that neighbouring dumps of Army Service Corps supplies got a bad time. Every New Zealander considered himself in honour bound to "pinch" extra fodder for his horse, to supplement the light ration, so that dumps, even when under guard, were mysteriously depleted of large quantities of tibbin and grain. The more daring spirits aimed at liberally supplementing their own rations as well, and resorted to many ingenious devices towards this end; particularly when such sought-after supplies as condensed milk and rum were known to exist in a nearby dump in any quantity.

The matter of the guard had to be considered — if they could not be "squared" they must be bluffed. The writer knows of one instance in which the guard on the dump at El Arish were Scotties—always the friends of the New Zealanders. Two mounted riflemen, cheery souls, who had "inside information" as to the contents of the dump, engaged the Scottish sentry in talk one evening. After some time a mutual agreement was entered into, the gist of which was, that the descent on the rum known to exist in cases nearby, should coincide with the moment that the sentry reached the most distant point of his beat. This arrangement worked satisfactorily, and the two adventurers each succeeded in getting clear with a fat, heavy case of promising appearance. After having carried the two cases, with much exertion, perhaps two miles along the beach, suspicions arose regarding their contents, and the foragers decided to sample them. Breaking both cases open, great was their disgust to find them containing a compressed dry ration of uninviting appearance, instead of the cheering liquid in jars that they had hoped for.

A trick practised with success by a Colonial horseman one day whilst working with others in a fatigue party, handling stores at a dump, was rather well executed. Waiting till the eye of authority was elsewhere, he dropped a case of tinned milk on its corner "good and hard." His mates, who had been previously rehearsed in their part, quickly gathered the scattered tins from the broken case and concealed them in their clothes. Then, with the most innocent air in the world, and a punctilious salute to the English officer in charge of the dump, this unblinking rascal asked, and obtained, permission to take away the smashed case "he had found" for firewood!

While at El Arish, a "de-lousing" parade was held. These parades were held at odd times when opportunities offered, and were often most amusing. All of a man's wearing apparel, and his blanket, would be put in big batches into a steam disinfector. There it would remain for about twenty minutes, when it would be supposed to be cleared of lice or other vermin — the writer one day heard a man remark that this treatment merely "refreshed them!" The steam disinfectors were either portable, or if on the railway, closed iron cars fitted with shelves and supplied with steam from an old engine.

On this day at El Arish, numbers of men

had stripped, and were waiting in most airy attire beside their horses until their clothing should be "cooked." Suddenly a "Jacko" aeroplane appeared, which shortly afterwards dropped a bomb not far from the disinfector. Then ensued a scene that baffles description, as men in all stages of deshabille, from a shirt to nothing at all, sprang on to their horses and scattered for their lives in all directions. It is perhaps superfluous to add that the humour of the situation was only appreciated afterwards.

Something should be said of the work of the Egyptian Labour Corps in this campaign. Thousands of natives, conscripted for terms of a few months, from Egypt, were constantly employed on railway construction. Without this native labour it would have been impossible to have pushed the railway across the Desert in rear of the troops as was done. When their term of service expired, they could be seen going down the line singing and waving flags like children, as the train bore them towards their homes. As one lot returned to Egypt, their places would be filled by others, and so, throughout the operations, a big body of these natives was constantly at work.

During construction work at El Arish, an enemy aeroplane came over one day. On the sounding of the aeroplane alarm, a mob of these natives made a dive for the shelter of a cutting. The Turk dropped a bomb fairly in the midst of them, killing twenty-seven, and making a horrible mess.

The British surveyors were enterprising, and mapped out the course the line was to take miles ahead of the construction gangs, under the protection of patrols and posts thrown out beyond the British main positions. In parts the Turkish patrols would often remove their survey pegs during the night. Had they gone deeper, however, these smart "Jackoes" would have found that the real pegs, from which the levels were taken, were beneath the ones they made away with, these last being mere "blinds."

Chapter VII.

Moving out from El Arish on January 8th, 1917, in company with three other Mounted Brigades, a Brigade of Camels, one Brigade of Horse Artillery, and an Indian Mountain Battery, the New Zealanders advanced on Rafa, the Gateway to Palestine, and, since the fall of Magh Daba, the most important Southern outpost of the Turks.

Marching all night, and covering a distance of over thirty miles, the Brigade got into position north-east of Rafa soon after dawn, when an attack on the prominent redoubt commenced from three sides. Early in the operation, some New Zealanders captured a German officer who was trying to make his way to the main Turkish position. He was found to speak excellent English, and so was haled before a well-known colonel for interrogation. During this process, one of his remarks was—"I know you have good troops, but you'll never take the redoubt." To which the New Zealand colonel, noted for his quick manner of speaking, replied in a breath—"Huh, all right, we'll see—we're going to have a go—tell you later on!" Later, under guard at Divisional Headquarters, this German was genuinely amazed to hear that the New Zealanders had taken the redoubt he thought impregnable, and, his professional interest no doubt thoroughly aroused, began to ask all sorts of questions about these wonderful troops from the ends of the earth who had accomplished the impossible. This incident is recounted as giving an indication of what was before our men as they went into action that morning at Rafa, where they acquitted themselves so well.

The country being open and only slightly undulating, the attack had to be developed dismounted, over ground devoid of all cover, and fully commanded by the heavily entrenched redoubt held by the Turks. The New Zealanders dismounted for action in some slight hollows, which only gave partial cover for the horses, some two thousand yards from their objective.

The attack on Rafa is to this day held up as a brilliant example of the support to advancing troops that can be given by overhead covering fire from machine-guns, which on this occasion kept the Turkish parapets in a continual haze of dust with accurately placed fire, and allowed our men to advance over open country in a way that would have otherwise been quite impossible.

The attack reached a stage in which it was held up by the withering fire poured in by the Turks holding the big redoubt. From their entrenched position they swept the open ground our men had to cross with a storm of fire against which there was no cover. The New Zealanders by this time were within easy range, and were being subjected to enfilade fire from a small isolated redoubt where the Turks had a machine-gun post. The other troops engaged were completely held up, and one unit had already acted upon orders to withdraw. To retire over such open ground under heavy enemy fire at this critical stage of the attack was out of the question for the New Zealand Brigade. It was therefore decided to push home the attack on the main Turkish positions as rapidly as possible. This was done, many casualties being sustained in the last phase of the advance, which culminated in a brilliant charge under a hail of fire over the last two hundred yards, and hand to hand fighting in the Turkish trenches. The defence then quickly collapsed, and the New Zealand Brigade were sole masters of the redoubt, with a big haul of prisoners and several guns.

At both Magh Daba and Rafa the Turks were more or less surprised by the sudden appearance of our troops before their positions at dawn. Their scouting aeroplanes in each case had been able to report the British forces in bivouac thirty miles away, over country which could be traversed but slowly, at sundown, but in each case our mounted troops accomplished the long journey during the hours of darkness.

The difficulties in evacuating the wounded throughout this campaign were often considerable, and it is worth while here to recount some of the hardships that attended men wounded in these engagements far from railhead.

At Rafa the action terminated at about five o'clock in the evening, but it was about eleven o'clock at night before the wounded were got away in sand-carts; these were two-wheeled hooded carts, fitted with broad tyres for travelling in the sand. The advanced casualty clearing station was at Sheik Zowaid, about eight miles away, the journey taking four hours over a rough track. Here the wounded men received the attention that very limited supplies and conveniences allowed; leaving next morning at about eleven o'clock they made the journey back to El Arish, a distance of nineteen slow miles, in cacolets slung one on each side of a camel. These cacolets were shallow box-like affairs made of wood and canvas, and travelling in them, with the continual rocking motion from side to side as the camel slouched along, was an excruciatingly painful experience for men badly wounded or with broken bones. This instance is merely typical of other occasions of a like nature, the agony of the journey to hospital often proving fatal to men severely wounded. From El Arish casualties would travel by stages down the line by hospital trains, through various hospitals, until a base hospital in Cairo was reached.

It was at Rafa that the New Zealanders realized the Desert Campaign was ended, and they stood on the threshold of Palestine. For the first time their eyes, accustomed to the fierce glare of the desert sand, beheld country covered with a tinge of green — the soil, although sandy, was in many places cultivated and under young crop, chiefly barley. Needless to say, the horses were not long in appreciating this fact, and eagerly nibbled at the welcome tufts of green, that reminded them, doubtless, of many a green homestead paddock in far off New Zealand. The sand decreased as the troops moved northwards, until later, near Gaza, our men travelled over rich black soil many feet deep.

Soon after the capture of Rafa, the Third Australian Brigade of Light Horse was detached from the Anzac Mounted Division, which, from that time onwards, consisted only of the 1st and 2nd Brigades of Australian Light Horse, and the New Zealand Brigade.

After the capture of Rafa, the Brigade moved back to El Arish, and later up to Sheik Zowaid, where their task was again that of covering the advance of the quickly moving railhead. During this work there were one or two engagements of a minor nature in the course of clearing Turkish posts in the vicinity of Khan Yunis. This was a picturesque township a few miles North of Rafa, possessing a tower that is a relic of the Crusades, in a fanciful setting of trees and high cactus hedges.

The Brigade subsequently established a bivouac at Rafa, from which place they set out to do their part in the first attack on Gaza. After the battle they retired to Belah.

While in these parts the New Zealanders had many experiences with the Bedouins, the camps of these wandering nomad Arabs dotting the countryside in brown and black clusters in all directions. Our men were to meet these natives throughout their travels in Palestine in greater numbers than the few half-starved Bedouins they had encountered in the Desert, and were to learn to their own cost what scoundrels they were. On the morning of the Rafa fight, a few of our men were detailed to gather in the Bedouins, whose camps, dotted all over the country, stood in the path of our advance.

Two men engaged in this work approached a large tent before which stood a fierce-looking Bedouin, evidently resenting this interference with his liberty. One trooper's attention being occupied for a moment, the Arab suddenly produced an ancient sabre from the folds of his voluminous clothing, and struck the other man on the head from behind, knocking him out. By the time his companion realized what had happened, the Bedouin had seized the bandolier and rifle of the prostrate man, and, vaulting on to his horse, had galloped away.

Unfortunately for the robber, this New Zealander was a noted shot. Taking careful aim, at a range of nearly eight hundred yards, he fired at the galloping horseman. The horse fell in a cloud of dust, throwing his rider clear. Being unhurt, the Bedouin commenced to run, when the marksman, deliberately reloading and aiming, brought him to his end with his second shot.

Periodically pitching their rude tents in different parts of the country, these Bedouins till and sow a small area of land with just enough seed to supply them with grain for their own use; in addition to which they had a few head of stock, mostly sheep and goats. The grain is garnered at harvest time, and ground up by the women into "doora," a coarse flour, which, when prepared, forms, with the milk from their goats, their staple articles of diet.

The wool from their few ragged sheep is spun by the women into a coarse yarn, which they weave on primitive hand looms into long strips of the roughest woollen cloth, resembling sacking. This, or sheepskins cured with the wool on, go to form their warmest clothing, under which they can be seen shivering in the rainy season. These strips of woollen cloth are also sewn together to form the long low tents under which they live, usually in conditions of the greatest filth.

Families, fowls, dogs, and often a donkey or two, live under the one shelter, which serves for every purpose, including cooking, and would make a sanitary inspector's hair stand on end.

The women are seldom seen away from their tents, but the men prowl abroad armed with an ancient sword or gun, often with knives in their belts, intent on thieving or other nefarious schemes.

They are of no use to their fellow men, producing nothing beyond that barely essential to their own needs, and on many occasions were suspected of carrying information to the Turks of British movements. They will do anything for material gain, a little loot or "baksheesh," and on more than one occasion were directly responsible for the deaths of New Zealanders. It may be said that the deaths of our men were amply avenged before the Brigade finally left Palestine.

"Standing to" in a wady during operations.

Turkish officers captured in the Beersheba operations.

CHAPTER VIII.

The next big adventure in which the New Zealand Mounted Rifle Brigade was concerned was the first attack on Gaza, the scene of many battles throughout history. In this attack, for the first time in the Campaign, the infantry in the British forces took a prominent part, the main attack on the town with its adjoining hill of Ali Muntar being left in their hands.

As the operations commenced, the New Zealanders moved round to the east of Gaza, the task assigned to them being chiefly that of preventing reinforcements reaching the enemy from the direction of Hareira and Beersheba, which our men successfully fulfilled. When the infantry attack failed, and they were in a difficult situation attempting to withdraw, the whole of the mounted troops were moved to the rear of Gaza. There they opened an attack on the Turkish positions in an endeavour to draw off the pressure from the British infantry, which by this time were in a bad plight. This having been in some measure accomplished, the mounted troops broke off the engagement, and at nightfall made a difficult withdrawal. The New Zealanders eventually reached Belah, after a gruelling time.

During the attack on the rear of Gaza, an incident occurred which typifies colonial resource, and may be briefly described. Some of the Wellington Regiment reached a few buildings on the outskirts of the town, a non-commissioned officer and section of men capturing two Turkish guns. This little party was under heavy fire from some Turks in a nearby building; the two guns being handy, these worthies decided to use one against the hostile building. None of the men knew anything of the working of a field piece, but, inspired by the non-commissioned officer, they backed the trail of the gun against a telegraph post, sighted it by the somewhat unusual expedient of looking through the barrel, and successfully loaded it. On pulling the firing lever the recoil of the gun knocked the telegraph post over, but the shell hit its target and broke up the Turks in the building with good effect. These two guns were brought out of action with considerable difficulty when the Brigade retired.

It should here be commented upon that this first attack on Gaza was an attack on the town alone. It was thought that if Gaza were taken Beersheba would become untenable by the Turks. After this unsuccessful venture a considerable extension of the British front to the right occurred. Thus the second attack on Gaza was concerned not only with the town, but with the line held by the Turks from Gaza to Beersheba, this also being a failure.

It may be remembered that the first attack on Gaza was reported in the press as a British success. After the British withdrawal an enemy aeroplane dropped a message which said, "You beat us at communiqués, but we beat you at Gaza."

The casualties to our forces in the two Gaza fights were said, unofficially, to total seventeen thousand. However this may be, it is certain that they were very much more severe than the authorities allowed the British public to believe at the time. The huge graveyard in Gaza to-day bears silent testimony to the costliness of both these efforts.

The historic town of Gaza itself stands on a gentle eminence, the white walls and quaint domed roofs of the city showing up through the green foliage of orchards and palm trees. To the West it is flanked by the sand dunes of the coast, to the East by the famous hill of Ali Muntar, which commands a wide stretch of country, and was the key to the Turkish defences. It was to this hill that Samson carried the gates of the city in Biblical times.

Before the War Gaza possessed a population of 40,000 inhabitants, but, during the long drawn out fighting for the possession of the town, almost the entire population deserted it. It is worth recording that since its capture, the greater part of the population has returned, and the place, under British administration, is rapidly returning to a thriving condition once more.

The modern town is much smaller than in ancient times, many of the present-day buildings containing material taken from old structures fallen into decay. The Turks damaged the place badly, ripping out most of the woodwork they could find for use as firewood or revetting material for their trenches before the town. They also stored ammunition in the great mosque in the centre of the city, which, on being detonated, caused considerable damage to the buildings around. The dominating minaret of this mosque afforded an ideal observation station for the Turks, so it was soon demolished by the British, one direct hit with a heavy shell bringing the tower down in a heap of wreckage. With the damage caused by shellfire the town was for a long time in ruins, but is now rapidly becoming habitable again. The town is the centre of a fertile barley-growing district, which cereal before the War was exported to England in large quantities for brewing into English beer. In olden times it was a scene of much trade and traffic, several of the chief caravan routes of the country leading to or through it. It was at Gaza that Samson exerted his strength to the detriment of the local temple, and literally brought down the house.

Between this first unsuccessful attempt to take Gaza and the second attempt on the town which occurred on April 19th, the New Zealand Brigade was employed on outpost and patrol work in the direction of Beersheba; this place was an important Turkish railhead, on the inland flank of the enemy's line. The opposing lines before Gaza were entrenched, but, as they ran inland into hilly country, were held in a series of posts and redoubts. The British right flank was very open, it being the special duty of the mounted troops to guard these wide open spaces.

Towards the middle of April, 1917, the New Zealanders moved out from Belah into the vicinity of Shellal, some miles inland, as part of a scheme to attempt to draw some of the opposing forces out from the defences of the town. Preparations for the second attack busily occupied our men, these including road-making over difficult crossings in the Wady Ghuzze, the big water-course which here divides the country in scarred and serried banks on its way to the sea, but which at this time was dry. One regiment was employed in the preparation of a reserve water supply, at Tel El Jemmi, in the Wady Ghuzze. Water was carried in fanatis by long strings of camels from Belah, miles away, one squadron in the course of a day's work filling sixty thousand gallons from these small tanks into large canvas cisterns in the Wady.

The second battle of Gaza lasted over three days, the infantry once more attacking the town. The New Zealand Brigade was sent in on the right flank of the attack, at Attawena, about eight miles inland from Gaza. The Turks held all the predominating positions, and although our men succeeded in evicting the enemy from their foremost trenches, their superiority in numbers and weight of artillery prevented the attack from being driven home, and compelled the withdrawal of the Brigade after dark.

The infantry attack also failed, so that Gaza still remained in Turkish hands. The New Zealand Brigade may be said to have attained in some degree what was required of them, in that they held to their sector of the line a big body of enemy troops, much their superior in numbers. The line held by the enemy at this time was a naturally strong one, of commanding positions. The Turks also possessed a big advantage in the railway line running to Beersheba behind their lines. This enabled them to quickly move troops from one part of their line to another, to any point that was threatened, whereas the British troops were attacking over difficult country with poor lines of communication.

After taking part in this second abortive attack on the stronghold of the Turks in Southern Palestine, in which the British casualties, including those of the New Zealand Brigade, were so very severe, the New Zealand unit moved back to Fara, on the Wady Ghuzze. Here our men were at once employed digging trenches, during a wave of intense heat, in view of a possible counter-attack by the enemy.

Then ensued a long period of patrol and outpost work, most of the reconnaissance being in the direction of Hareira and Beersheba, both of which places were by this time swarming with Turkish troops. These "stunts," although of a minor nature in the whole scheme of operations, were very trying on the men who performed them. A man would be on patrol one day, starting with the usual "stand-to" about three o'clock in the darkness before dawn, travelling over arid, dusty country all day, and not returning till after dark. Outpost duty would claim him the next night, to be followed, if he were lucky, by a spell of sorts the next day. Then the cycle of duty would commence again, this routine continuing week after week.

Many fond parents would have failed to recognize their sons could they have seen them returning from patrol duty in those times. As the troop rode into bivouac with a jingling of accoutrements, some men would be seen wearing riding breeches, others slacks, with their spurs. Their bodies would be but half covered in sleeveless shirts or singlets, always open at the neck, round which was slung the heavy bandolier. Rifles would be carried across the front of the saddle or slung over the left shoulder. Many would be unshaven, with red-rimmed eyes peering from faces darkened by sunburn and dust. The horses' coats would be rough and streaked with sweat, and horse and rider would be smothered in the dust of the day's march. The slouch hats worn by the men of the troop would vie with each other in disreputable appearance—if there had been no issue of fresh headgear for some time, many would have the crown half off like a flapping lid, the lower part being adorned by a ragged puggaree. For all their rough appearance, however, such a troop of apparent ruffians could always be depended on when it came to business—as the Turks well knew to their cost. The rough exterior covered hearts of gold, and as the little cavalcade rode in, the day's work done, no matter how tiring it had been, there would always be some irrepressible wag raising smiles by his apt comments on life in general and those around him in particular.

It was while the New Zealanders were in this locality that a mosaic floor of great historical interest was discovered on a small hill on the bank of the Wady Ghuzze. It was found in the course of excavating a small emplacement for a machine-gun, and was later carefully taken up and sent down the line to safer quarters.

The Turks at this time had distinctly "got their tails up" after the two British reverses at Gaza, and frequently tried to scupper the New Zealand patrols. There was a hill nearby, from which the adventures of these small parties of horsemen on the open country below could be watched by their mates; the frequent gatherings there, to watch the patrol encounters on the country beneath them, gave this area of flying shots and galloping horses the nickname of "the racecourse."

The heat of the summer was being felt at this time, and thick dust lay everywhere. The routine of watering the horses twice daily was an unpleasant business, involving, as it did, a ride of some length in a blinding, suffocating, cloud of dust, through which a man could but dimly perceive the horse ahead of him.

The stay at Fara was interrupted for a time, some weeks after the second battle of Gaza, by a demolition expedition to the Turkish railway near Asluj, which ran towards Magh Daba. The New Zealanders on this occasion formed part of a column consisting of the Anzac Division, with the Imperial Camel Corps in support. A many-arched and substantial stone railway viaduct was completely demolished with explosives, several miles of line being destroyed in the same way, thus isolating what remained intact of the railway to the south. The object of the demolition was the destruction of material, which the Turks might otherwise have taken up and relaid behind their lines.

On the 18th of August, 1917, the Brigade left Fara for a fortnight on the beach near Khan Yunis—from there they returned to El Fukhari, not a great distance from Fara, where they remained until the historic advance on Beersheba commenced on the night of October 28th. While at El Fukhari, a party of men was detailed to ride over to the railway and take delivery of some six hundred donkeys for the Anzac Division. Arrived at the station, the men set about unloading the bored-looking quadrupeds with their comical expressions and long floppy ears. Then the fun began, as this strange column started on its road. The donks were tied in fives, and travelled mostly in circles. First would be one man with the four horses of each section—behind him would be the other three men of the section—each vainly striving to make an erring team of five donkeys travel on the road instead of touring the surrounding country. It was finally decided to loosen the little wretches and try driving them like a mob of sheep. This was done, but the experiment was not a success—there appeared to be white donkeys all over Palestine as they perversely scattered out into the country round about. They had to be rounded up and caught again, which took some time and ingenuity. The procession continued, until the party arrived with their charges at Headquarters. There they handed over the "new remounts"—as an amused crowd of bystanders called them.

These donks were distributed amongst the various units, about seven to a squadron, and were ridden or led by "spare parts."

The official reason for their appearance was the shortage of remounts, but the ultimate purpose for which they were intended became evident later on, after the capture of Jerusalem.

Then the hardy little animals were called in, and thousands of them were used in "donkey trains" transporting supplies over the rough tracks and steep grades of the Judean Hills.

Needless to say, when the Brigade was in bivouac, the donks were at times the cause of much amusement in races, and "polo,"—played with walking sticks and a football!

Chapter IX.

A description of the way our men used to lay out a bivouac when occupying new ground may interest the reader. A soldier's home is under his hat, and this was literally true of our men, who never knew rest billets in buildings, but had to rig up what shelters they could wherever the Brigade halted. Let it be said here that, hot as the days are in Palestine, the nights are usually cold, making a man value every shred of cover. In laying out a bivouac, when the nature of the ground allowed of it, in most cases the three squadrons composing a regiment, the regimental transport, and headquarters, would be placed some distance apart from each other. The object of this was to present only a scattered target for enemy aeroplane bombs.

The horses were usually placed either in two parallel lines for each squadron, or in one long line, perhaps with an angle in it, this latter method being thought by some to offer the poorest target of all to aeroplanes. Each man carried on his horse a picketing or "built-up" rope, in addition to his headrope. This "built-up" rope was about five feet in length, having a wooden toggle at one end and a spliced loop at the other, which enabled the ropes of a whole squadron, if necessary, to be joined into one long line. The line of picketing ropes thus formed was stretched along the ground, and the extremities anchored down securely, by means of sacks filled with earth or sand, sunk below ground level. After this, the line was held down in each section of four ropes by sandbags let into the ground in similar manner. This system was first used in the Desert, where pegs would not hold, and was found to be most effective for security.

The men's "bivvies" (as their crude, often weirdly erected, but always practical, shelters of blankets or canvas were called), were generally put up in line in rear of the horse-lines, a space being left in between for saddlery and other gear.

Until quite late in the campaign the only shelters the men had were such as they could improvise from blankets and canvas, with the exception of a few bivouacs, where a limited number of tents was allotted them. Then they were supplied with canvas bivouac sheets, one to each man.

These were about six feet square, with buttons and buttonholes along each margin. Two men buttoned their sheets together, supported them on two sticks, pegged down the lower edges, and tied a blanket round one open end, when they had a fairly serviceable little shelter. Enemy bivouac sheets were much sought after when captures were made, as these were made of excellent quality light canvas, with aluminium buttons, superior to ours.

In a bivouac likely to be occupied for some time, it was a common practice to dig a narrow trench inside the tiny shelter. This allowed room for the legs when sitting on the narrow ledge on each side which served for a bunk, and in emergency formed a useful "funk hole" below the level of the whirring bomb fragments during an aeroplane raid. Cooking was done just outside the bivvy on a few stones or bully beef tins. Many would dig out a shallow trench nearby, leaving a square block of earth standing in the centre, which served as a table for meals.

The section of four men being the smallest working unit of a mounted regiment, one man generally attended to the commissariat, and did the cooking and tea-making in mess-tins and billies, while the other three looked after the four or more horses. The co-operation, consideration for each other, and unselfishness, shown by our men in sharing their work and dangers in the field, would be a revelation to many people at home, and was one of the finest features of life in the New Zealand Mounted Rifle Brigade in the memory of the writer. Newcomers in reinforcement drafts reaching the Brigade for the first time quickly had selfishness knocked out of them, and, under the rough chaff and good-humoured patience of their experienced comrades, quickly learnt the necessity of co-operation in all things, and the valuable lesson of always helping others besides themselves.

In each squadron there were, in addition to riding horses, twelve pack-horses—four Hotchkiss gunpacks, two Hotchkiss ammunition packs, four tool packs on which were carried picks and shovels, and two squadron packs for various uses; so that with these, and spare horses, of which there were always many when a squadron was not up to strength, or had recently had casualties, a big proportion of the men had to look after two, and sometimes three horses.

Practice makes perfect, and it was wonderful to see how quickly one of the New Zealand Mounted Rifle Regiments could settle down for the night when on trek, or moving into a new bivouac.

As soon as the bivouac area was allotted to a unit, the troops would move on to the ground, each squadron halting in the formation in which the lines were to be put down—usually column of half-squadrons.

On the order to dismount being given, built-up ropes would quickly be taken off the horses' necks and joined up into one long line. Then while the horseholders in each section looked after the horses, the remainder would set to work with pick, shovel, and bayonet to stretch and anchor down the horse lines. This done, the horses would be tied on the line, off-saddled, perhaps given an opportunity to roll, if the ground was soft, groomed, and then fed. The patient animals always knew the order "feed up," which was greeted with a chorus of hungry whinnyings and much pawing of the ground.

Then, and not till then, the men would set about making themselves as comfortable as circumstances allowed. Bivvies would spring up all over the area like magic, often supported, if sticks were scarce, on two bayoneted rifles, the bayonet being driven into the ground, while the butt of the rifle carried the canvas or blanket. As dusk fell, hundreds of tiny fires would flicker brightly in the gathering gloom, as shadowy figures moved about in preparation of the indispensable billy of tea to wash down "hard tack" and "bully."

On many "stunts," when it was necessary to travel as lightly as possible, bivouac sheets or blankets could not be carried, and then all hands had to sleep under no other canopy than the twinkling stars—quite all right in fine weather, but a miserable experience in the rainy season.

After the evening "boil-up," rations for the following day for horse and man would be drawn if the transport waggons had arrived, otherwise early next morning, or whenever opportunity offered. Water-bottles would also be filled on the arrival of the water-cart, these welcome vehicles often having to cover long distances to procure the necessary water for drinking. Horse pickets for the night would be detailed, two men per squadron having to watch

Austrian troops evacuating Jerusalem before the tide of the British advance. (Captured enemy photograph.)

The N.Z.M.R. formally taking possession of Jaffa. The ceremony at the Town Hall.

over the horses in two-hour reliefs through the night, so that ten or twelve men would be on this duty nightly. This essential routine having been performed, and many other affairs attended to, such as stripping required gear from carefully packed saddles, the weary soldiers would turn in with what measure of comfort they could secure on the hard bosom of mother earth.

In the morning the bivouac would be astir before dawn, the pale light of the coming day revealing saddled horses and ground devoid of bivouacs. Everywhere would be men rolling blankets, strapping gear to saddles, and tying up and securing their horses' canvas nosebags.

On the warning "get ready to move," straps and girths would be finally tightened, and horses bitted up, until punctually at the appointed time the leading squadron would move out mounted. This would be followed by the remainder in ordered succession, as the long column of sun-browned horsemen, with the regimental transport waggons in rear, streamed away on the day's march in a cloud of enveloping dust.

When the Brigade was on a "stunt" and in the vicinity of the enemy, the routine described would not be so peaceful, but would be varied by long trying nights on outpost, the horses remaining saddled and the men getting but a brief snatch of sleep between turns on sentry or horse-piquet. Or, as generally happened, the Brigade would march all night, the tiring ride often culminating in a collision with the enemy at dawn.

This might be merely a small affair concerning the advance guard, or might develop into an action in which the whole force would be engaged.

On many occasions, when the mounted column was travelling over country impassable for wheeled traffic, the transport waggons of the three regiments, the machine-gun squadron, and the field ambulance, would be brigaded, and travel in a separate column by a different route more easily traversed, meeting the Brigade later at the next bivouac.

In the many bivouacs occupied in different parts of Palestine by our men for periods of a few weeks on end, a marquee or two was erected to house the Brigade canteen. This was instituted shortly after the New Zealanders first entered Palestine, and under energetic management proved a great boon to the men, providing, as it did, tinned fruit, fish, milk, sugar, tea, tobacco, and other goods at the most reasonable prices possible. It was especially appreciated in the closing phases of the campaign, when rations were cut down and hardships were considerable.

CHAPTER X.

When the advance on Beersheba commenced, the New Zealand Mounted Rifle Brigade formed part of the swiftly moving column that executed the brilliant turning movement at Beersheba, and allowed the thrust at Gaza to be made, which this time was completely successful. Down the ages of history, Gaza has been the scene of many battles, but was probably never subjected to such a battering as the town received on the occasion of this third attack by the British. The artillery bombardment was terrific, and greatly facilitated the work of the storming infantry.

The New Zealand Mounted Rifle Brigade left El Fukhari on the evening of the 25th October, and, marching all night, arrived early next morning at Essani, fifteen miles away. There the New Zealanders stayed three days, acting in support of yeomanry and supplying escorts for camel trains. Leaving Essani on the night of the 28th, they rode due south to Khalassa, a distance of about ten miles. Resting all day after their arrival in the morning they marched again at night, in dense clouds of dust, to Asluj, another fifteen miles. Here was encountered the first metalled road since leaving the Suez

Canal, and the Turkish narrow-gauge railway.

Such night marches as these, a common experience of the Mounted men, will live long in their memories. Usually moving off at dusk, the long column takes the road in the enveloping dust which always shrouds the movement of a mounted column in Palestine in the dry season. Little is heard beyond the shuffling of the horses' feet and the jingle and rattle of accoutrements—the clink of stirrups and bits or perhaps the rattle of a mess-tin or some equipment on a pack-saddle loosely tied on. Occasional disjointed remarks are heard — perhaps to do with a load on some horse requiring adjustment — or a speculation as to the destination — then perhaps the curt order, "No Smoking!" — but for the most part the column pushes its way on through the darkness in almost complete silence. A sudden slowing up of the horses in front and figures dimly seen dismounting means a few minutes' halt, when the tired riders stretch themselves on the ground alongside their horses, sublimely indifferent to the risk of being kicked or trodden on. Often the weary steeds, with almost human understanding, lie down beside their riders to rest their aching legs.

A sound of movement in front and the brief rest is at an end as each man climbs into his saddle on the order "get mounted" being passed down from the head of the column as it commences to move again. So the march continues throughout the night with occasional halts. Some men fall asleep in their saddles and are carried on in uneasy oblivion by their understanding mounts — others remain awake in a world of moving shadows and distorted images.

The early morning hours of darkness are the most trying, for then vitality is at its lowest and fatigued bodies ache all over. Then comes the first lightening of the eastern sky, and the new day dawns with a cheering influence, which is increased as the next halt gives the opportunity for a hurried "boil-up" of tea; after which things seem not so bad after all to the dust-smothered and unshaven warriors.

At Asluj water for the horses was very short, and the long trek continued again that evening. During the night the Brigade covered a distance of some thirty-six miles, moving in a triple column composed of mounted troops, artillery, and transport, on a road barely half a chain wide.

In the morning the sequel to this fatiguing night was an action against the Turks holding the Tel El Saba redoubt, east of Beersheba. This fight at Saba was typical of the way in which an attack was developed from the time the first shots were fired at the advance guard. The Turkish main positions were on the summit of a hill which from its dominating position formed one of the chief keys to the defence of Beersheba. Auckland Regiment made the attack, in conjunction with the 2nd Australian Light Horse Brigade, the other New Zealand Regiments continuing the sweeping movement on their right which was to culminate in the fall of Beersheba. The thin line of scouts riding in the screen were held up by enemy fire at a range of about two thousand yards. They dismounted and at once replied in an endeavour to pick up the range. Their thin line was then reinforced by the troops acting in support of them, and then further strengthened as the remainder of the regiment behind deployed and came into action dismounted.

The line then commenced to move forward, first one part advancing covered by the fire of the others, then another section. The ground, being more or less broken, afforded fairly good cover, but the Turkish artillery made good shooting and put over many good bursts of shrapnel which whipped the ground amongst the advancing New Zealanders into myriad spurts of dust. The engagement thus developed until the attacking line was perhaps two or three hundred yards from the Turks, when heavy fire was exchanged from both sides. Then the New Zealanders charged with fixed bayonets, pushing the attack home with great determination as they mounted the rising ground towards the enemy. The sight of the cold steel coming upon them was evidently too much for the morale of the Turks, for their fire died down as our panting men approached their trenches, and those that did not bolt soon surrendered. Thus was another victory added to the record of the New Zealand Mounted Rifle Brigade.

In the well executed movement by the British forces which resulted in the fall of Beersheba, the long detour made by our mounted troops led the Turks to believe that the main attack was to be delivered in this vicinity. This resulted in their fatal error of moving troops from their coastal flank into the hills near Beersheba, thus enabling the British troops to smash through at Gaza and in other parts of the line.

After the fall of Beersheba, the Brigade was engaged at Ras El Nagb, northwards in the direction of Hebron, against these enemy troops. The country was hilly and difficult, the result being that the New Zealanders (as happened a number of times during the Campaign) came under heavy artillery fire from the Turks, with no support from British guns. The Turks attempted to dislodge Canterbury Regiment from their positions by a bayonet charge, but were beaten off, although in the five days or so that our men were engaged in this locality this Regiment suffered very severe casualties.

The relieving troops were late in arriving, the New Zealanders being a day or two almost without water or rations—so that with this and the strain of the fighting our men were about "all in" when they were finally relieved. It took them all their time to march back the five miles or so to the horses on foot, over the rough stony ground.

Whilst fighting in this part, water for the horses could not be found, and these animals performed a wonderful feat of endurance in existing without it for seventy-two hours—in the case of one waggon team eighty-four hours. They were eventually led back to Beersheba and watered there, a distance of twelve miles.

The New Zealand Brigade was then withdrawn from this area, and rationed up at Beersheba, whence they marched through Hareira and Huj to Ascalon. In this trek our men covered a distance of over sixty miles in thirty-six hours, with only two spells en route; a fine performance for weary horses and men, when it is considered that they were then fully rationed, and carrying the maximum load, which has previously been shown was no light weight.

Slightly north of Ascalon, the New Zealanders encountered the first of the many large orange groves which dot the countryside in vivid green patches near Jaffa. On the 14th of November, they came into sanguinary collision with the Turks at a place called Ayun Kara, about nine miles south of Jaffa.

The fight occurred on open, undulating ground with no cover, and our men got no opportunity of entrenching themselves. Auckland Regiment held the left, Wellington the centre, and Canterbury the right, the Brigade being attacked by a whole Turkish division with the evident intention of wiping them out. The Turks charged with fixed bayonets, and endeavoured to turn the New Zealanders' left flank, towards the sandhills of the coast. Their attack was thus heaviest against Auckland and Wellington, the brunt of it falling on Auckland.

The Turks got to within bomb-throwing distance, but were eventually beaten off in the last thirty or forty yards of their advance, after a fierce struggle, in which our men fought like tigers. Casualties on both sides were very heavy, most of the grim combat occurring at very short range, some of our men being put out of action with hand grenades. Only the grim determination of the New Zealanders and their unwavering, deadly markmanship with rifle, machine-gun, and Hotchkiss rifle stopped the Turkish rush before it overwhelmed them. The fight ranged at close quarters for some time in the fiercest intensity, and then as the tide of battle turned, the remnant of the attacking Turks withdrew in disorder, leaving our men as victors in a frightful shamble of dead and wounded. Throughout that night our thin line of survivors held on to their positions ready for any renewed attack by the enemy, the darkness being made horrible by the groans and cries of the wounded Turks lying before our line. The early morning light revealed a field littered with corpses, some four hundred Turkish dead being counted before Auckland's position alone. When it is remembered that a mounted rifle regiment dismounts for action only a little over two hundred men, and that the Regiment was far from full strength, the eighty-nine casualties suffered by Auckland give some indication of the fierceness of the engagement. There were probably not more than one hundred and thirty or one hundred and forty men in the line, and yet, with their heavy percentage of casualties, these great-hearted men from peaceful New Zealand accounted for a huge roll of enemy dead, over and above wounded.

The following essay, which was written by a Jewish schoolgirl in Richon Le Zion, shows the relief with which our occupation of the pretty little hamlet was welcomed after the decisive battle of Ayun Kara, which took place barely a mile from the village.—

"For several days the roar of the guns became louder, gradually approaching our village. It seems almost incredible when we think that the British Army is coming soon, after three and a half years of patient waiting.

We were instructed by our late Turkish masters to stay strictly indoors during the awful conflict, so we were practically prisoners.

Presently news arrived that the British had occupied Dieran, and we thought they would reach here by the following day.

Wednesday morning heralded a fresh outburst of the artillery, much nearer to our settlement, and we thought that a big battle was raging not far from here; all day we were afraid of the frightful noise, but in the evening it ceased. Later on the Turkish troops began to enter the settlement. All ranks seemed completely tired and crestfallen, and the wounded were crying out for food and water. That night was dark and cold; the Turks wandered about the roads for a place to rest. We received orders to supply food for man and beast, and we all wondered where they were going to. Was it that the British Army was too powerful for them to resist it any longer?

About midnight they installed a telephone, which made us think they were going to stay and continue fighting next day.

Everybody in our house sat up all night thinking and suggesting what would occur on the morrow. I thought that we would be told to leave the place in the morning. We all dreaded the idea of leaving our homes, not knowing when we would be able to return. My sister and I, looking from our window, heard the confusion in the street below, but owing to the darkness we could see nothing. The cries of the wounded were pitiful. My brother-in-law had great confidence in the early appearance of the British troops, and he told us to have courage because to-morrow we would all be free. Afterwards he retired to sleep, but told me to awaken him if I heard any soldiers speaking English.

In the early hours of the morning the Turks began to depart, and by eight o'clock we had bade adieu to the last Turkish officer, and everybody rejoiced and waited patiently for the conquerors to arrive.

Everything was quiet, so we looked in all directions for the first sign of any British troops. Presently I heard my brother calling me, saying, "Come here, Rachel, and see the cavalry."

Taking the glasses with me, I distinctly saw a large body of horsemen approaching in our direction, and it seemed almost incredible for the British to have captured our colony from the Turks without our being molested or disturbed. My brother became excited and hastened away to greet the first of them. After ten minutes two New Zealand troopers rode up to us and spoke, but I was very sorry that I could not understand English.

Presently one man spoke to his companion, who smiled, and I have since learned that he said, "They are not bad looking girls about here."

Afterwards many troops came up, and all the civilians came out of their houses to welcome them. Everybody was overjoyed. The advance-guard stayed here all day, and that evening their Commanding Officer, General Meldrum, rode into the colony and interviewed the residents.

Looking from our balcony now and watching the street full of soldiers, it seems that our dream has at last come true, and we can already see visions of a new life free from Turkish misrule; and we shall try to forget the past and for a victorious peace we will drink "Palestine wine" in Palestine.

Now that the Turks have departed and the British (we hope) have come to stay, everybody in the colony is very busy learning the English language.

When the British first arrived only some people could understand them. I remember the first soldier who spoke to me—I could answer only by gestures, but now I am pleased to be able to speak and read a little.

Among the New Zealanders you will hear the Hebrew words "Shalom, Ma Shlemba, toda raba, etc." ("Good-day, how are you? Thank you very much, etc."). So both parties are fraternising and are becoming every day closer friends."

Chapter XI.

Soon after this decisive battle the New Zealand Brigade occupied Jaffa, on the coast, a town in normal times of about fifty thousand inhabitants, but at this time nearly deserted. As in the case of Gaza, the population rapidly grew once more upon the advent of British administration. The town possesses many fine buildings, and Sarona, a suburb to the north east, is well laid out and modern. The centre of the town occupies a gentle eminence overlooking the sea, the rest of it running north and south along a wide stretch of sea beach.

The legend of Andromeda and the sea monster is supposed to have originated on the rocks over which the waves break in its indifferent harbour, while Jonah is said to have had his adventure in the whale's tummy not far away. The house of Simon the tanner is another spot of historic interest which may be seen, or rather the site of it, for the original building has long since disappeared and been built over by a house of modern origin. Before the War Jaffa was the pilgrim port of Jerusalem, some fifteen to twenty thousand of these people passing through it annually.

The German Consulate in the town was occupied by New Zealand Brigade Headquarters, many New Zealanders (be it whispered) taking great delight in the use of the impressively headed official stationery which was found there in large quantities.

The country immediately surrounding the town is very fertile, and beautiful with vineyards and orange-groves, these latter being a great sight as the luscious fruit ripens goldenly against the vivid green of the trees. The abundance of oranges was appreciated to the full, and probably did much towards keeping our men fit.

It is worth recording that the New Zealand Mounted Rifle Brigade were the first troops to enter Jaffa, on the extreme left flank of the British line, and also, later, were amongst the first British troops to enter Jericho on the extreme right.

Soon after the occupation of Jaffa, the New Zealanders were engaged to the north of it, across the Auja river at Khirbet Hadra, and also at Sheik Muanis. The former event was nearly a disaster, the Turks once more attempting to finish our men off by an attack in overwhelming force one morning at dawn. The New Zealanders narrowly escaped being cut off by the river and mown down by heavy artillery and machine-gun fire. As it was the casualties were heavy enough, but the enemy's object of finally disposing of the dreaded "death-riders," as the Turks called the slouch-hatted Colonial horsemen, was not realized.

The suburb of Sarona, behind our men, largely inhabited by Germans, and at that time still containing many German women, was suspected of signalling or sending information of our strength on the northern bank of the river to the enemy, for the Turkish attack on this occasion was timed to catch the New Zealand unit at the maximum disadvantage, in a difficult and unsupported outpost position.

This suburb of Sarona contained a winepress, which our men soon discovered, and relieved by the simple process of syphoning the wine out of casks into water-bottles, or canvas water-buckets. Later, an English unit mounted a guard over the place, and the New Zealanders were sore perplexed at their free supply of wine being cut off. However, where there's a will there's a way.

One evening a well turned out New Zealand guard, with fixed bayonets, and commanded by a sergeant, marched up to the guard-room. With great éclat each guard paid the usual compliment of presenting arms. Then the sergeants conferred, the Tommy non-commissioned officer demurring that he had no orders about relief at that time. Such trifling objections the New Zealanders quickly over-ruled, soon convincing the Englishman that everything was in order. The sentry was relieved by a mounted rifleman, and after the usual return of compliments the old guard marched off.

A bivouac in the Jordan Valley.

Arabs in the employ of the British Intelligence.

New Zealanders crossing the Jordan after the first attack on Amman.

The New Zealand sentry remained on duty, but the rest of the bogus guard dived into the building, and quickly emerged with all they could carry. By the time outraged authority discovered the hoax, the last of our men were just disappearing in the distance with a heavy load—thus were the home fires (internal) kept burning!

On another occasion a well-known "hard case" in Canterbury Regiment was riding towards the wine-press one evening with his intentions quite evident by reason of the score or so of water-bottles slung round his own and his horse's anatomy. He was but slightly disconcerted to meet a well-known Assistant Provost Marshal, who stopped him with an enquiry as to where he was going. As he was on the direct track to the wine-press, evasion was useless, so "Up to the wine-press, sir," was the reply. "What for?" queried the officer. "To get some feed for my horse, sir," was the unsmiling answer—with which the worthy rode on before the officer had time to stay him.

During their stay in the vicinity of Jaffa, the New Zealanders for a time relieved the infantry in the trenches. This was rather a miserable experience, the weather being very cold and wet. The trench sides kept falling in, everyone becoming smothered in the sticky red mud, while the Turkish artillery was unpleasantly attentive.

Canterbury moving back first, Wellington and Auckland followed, and after a two days' trek arrived at Sukerier, on Christmas Day, 1917, in a teeming deluge of rain which soaked every man and his gear through and through. This bivouac was in the sandhills, on the coast just north of Esdud, or Ashdod, as the old maps call it. This is a typical native village of mud-walled houses with thatched roofs. In the rainy season these roofs are green with the growth of barley and other seeds which have germinated amongst the refuse thrown on them, and the whole village blends into the green tone of the surrounding country in a way that makes it almost invisible at a distance.

After a short stay near Esdud a move was made farther north, a bivouac being established at Ayun Kara, adjoining the battlefield where so many good men had "gone west," and the Jewish village of Richon Le Zion.

Here the Brigade had a well-earned spell for a few weeks while the units were refitted and brought up to strength. The nearby village of Richon is a pretty little hamlet surrounded by vineyards and orange-groves, where the Jewish inhabitants were keenly appreciative of our mens' work in the Ayun Kara fight, in freeing them from the yoke of the detested Turk. The centre of interest is the substantially built brick wine-press, with its huge cellars, the property of Rothschild, and one of the three largest wine-presses in the world. Light white and red wines and cognac could be had at reasonable prices, and were largely in demand.

The country in this part of Palestine consists of rolling downs, and, the soil being light and porous, it formed an excellent camping ground during the rainy season, the rest spell terminating all too soon. Keen interest was taken in football matches between the different units, and other sport. A few miles away was situated Ludd, which became an important railhead for the military railway, and in history as Lydda was associated with the exploits of St. George, the patron saint of England.

This village is situated picturesquely in a setting of olive trees and cactus hedges, on a fertile flat which under modern handling should yield heavily the fruits of agriculture. As with many parts of Palestine, the possibilities are there, and it will be interesting to see in the next few years what use is made of them.

Chapter XII.

First the Canterbury Regiment, and then Wellington, moved out for a tour of duty holding posts in the Judean foothills, and then the New Zealanders turned their horses' heads eastwards, and, joining up with Wellington en route, set out on a long trek to the right flank to take part in operations there, many miles inland. Leaving the cultivated land of the coast, the route led up into the stony hills of Judea, with their endless outcropping boulders. The road curved amongst the hills in country quite different from the downs of the coastal plain. The hills were masses of grey rock, here and there built into terraces for the cultivation of grapes in sunny aspects; in parts the harshness of the landscape was softened by the grey-green tints of olive trees.

The Brigade passed through Bethlehem, which witnessed the nativity of Christ, and where may be seen the large Church of the Nativity, which has passed through many vicissitudes in the course of history. Our men then threaded their way over precipitous mountain tracks eastwards towards the Valley of the Jordan.

It is interesting to record that the route followed through the hills on this occasion was the one traversed by Ruth in Biblical times. Having left the Hills of Moab she crossed the Jordan Valley, and made her way up this mountain track to Bethlehem, where she made such an impression on Boaz in the harvest fields.

The going in many parts was over steep, rocky paths, over which the horses had to be led in single file, the Brigade being strung out in a column perhaps five miles in length.

The Turks were encountered at Nebi Musa, (the burial-place of Moses according to the Moslems), and although they held commanding positions withdrew after a comparatively brief action.

Soon after this Jericho was occupied, the New Zealanders being amongst the first troops to enter the town. Our men were thus the successors, after long years, of Joshua, and mounted the first British guard in Jericho. When they first rode into the place, the priest rang the church bell, and the women, who were mostly on the housetops (the universal vantage point in times of excitement), sprinkled water on them from bottles. This last performance was not at all appreciated by some of the men, the general opinion being that the water would have been put to better use, with the addition of some soap, on the persons of the ladies (?) themselves. It afterwards transpired that these natives were doing what they considered great honour to the conquerors, the water used being from the River Jordan.

In the hospital our men found a number of dead and dying Turks, the dead still on beds alongside the living, with the usual neglect of the most elementary sanitary measures so characteristic of the Turks.

As with many other places in the Holy Land, Jericho proved to be disappointing in appearance. Instead of the town pictured in the imagination as having some dignity clinging to it by reason of its departed grandeur, our men found what is little more than a native village of the usual squalid type, with a few modern stone buildings. Some trees and vegetation make the surroundings green in the barren waste of the Jordan Valley, owing their existence to a fairly good water supply which originates in the Ain Es Sultan spring behind the town. According to an early tradition this was the water which Elisha healed with salt, whence it is called Elisha's Spring by Christians. Of the departed glory of Jericho, with its fine buildings and plantations of date palms and bananas, hardly a trace remains to the eye of the casual observer — such can be found only by archaeologists.

The modern natives of the place, only about three hundred in number, are of a very degenerate type, probably owing to the deadly climate, it being situated nearly a thousand feet below sea level and infested with malarial mosquitoes. The causes of the town's gradual decay are said to be chiefly attributable to misgovernment and malaria.

After the taking of Jericho, Canterbury and Wellington Regiments moved back to the bivouac at Ayun Kara, on the other side of the country, Auckland Regiment alone remaining in the Jordan Valley. This regiment was then engaged for some time in useful patrol work. So afraid were the Turks of the Colonial horsemen, that it was a common practice for them to ''snipe'' at our patrols with their field guns, often sending shell after shell over at a couple, or even one, of our men. As they often made exceptionally good practice at such moving targets, patrol work under direct observation was most exciting, as one shell crashed before a rider and another whipped up the dust behind him with its flying fragments.

Auckland Regiment helped in forcing the first crossing of the river Jordan by British troops. This crossing was made at the most famous ford of the Jordan, at Mahadet Hajleh, which is supposed to be the scene of the baptism of Christ. It is at this spot that the many pilgrims to the Jordan are dipped every year.

At the time the New Zealanders crossed it, however, in March, 1918, the river was filled from bank to bank, and was a swiftly running torrent many feet deep, the pontoon bridge over which the crossing was made being constructed by Pioneers under difficulties and heavy enemy fire. This regiment of mounted rifles was the first to clear the ground immediately east of the river of Turks, clearing several miles of country in a brilliant operation which resulted in the capture of ten machine-guns and a good haul of prisoners. During this "stunt" one troop put to flight a body of Turkish cavalry double their number, putting half of them out of action in killed and wounded. Such is Destiny that the only New Zealander killed was the brilliant young officer who led the troop, beloved of all. Auckland also did good work in seizing what was afterwards made the main bridgehead on the river, the Ghoraniyeh crossing, directly east of Jericho.

At Jericho the Jordan Valley is roughly twelve miles wide. From the towering Mount of Temptation, with Jericho below it, on the west, the country, which is flat or only slightly undulating, slopes gradually towards the river. Perhaps a mile from the stream, the ground becomes furrowed and gutted by deep gullies into chalky hills, through which the track winds uncertainly till the river is reached. On the eastern side of the river the first mile or so is cut up into chalky hills of all formations in the same manner, and then as the gullies become shallower the country runs up in a gradual slope, covered with thorny scrub, to the foot of the Mountains of Gilead.

The Jordan River, which runs from north to south, to empty itself into the Dead Sea, is of an average width of forty or fifty yards. It turns and twists, like a writhing snake, amidst a vividly green fringe of vegetation which shows up in strong contrast to the chalky hills around.

Chapter XIII.

Towards the end of March, Canterbury and Wellington Regiments again trekked across Palestine to the Jordan Valley, and, crossing the river at midnight on the light pontoon bridge, joined up with Auckland on the eastern bank of the river at dawn on March 24th. This was the morning after Auckland's successful day in clearing this ground of Turks.

The New Zealand Brigade now formed part of the force which was to attack Amman, on the Hedjaz railway. The objects of this operation were to effectually damage the Hedjaz railway, and, if possible, capture the town of Amman. The successful accomplishment of the former would have cut off forces of the enemy lower down the line, compelling them to submit to attack by the King of the Hedjaz, working in co-operation with the British. The capture of Amman itself would have been a big blow to the Turks, for this was their distributing point for this section of their front for troops and supplies as they came down from the north by rail.

The Hedjaz railway is a narrow-gauge line running from Damascus to Medina, a distance of about seven hundred miles. It is three quarters of an inch narrower in gauge than the New Zealand railways, the rails being laid on steel sleepers. The line is well engineered, and in parts winds up steep grades in a clever serpentine course. The locomotives used are very heavy and powerful, of German build. The line was originally built entirely for religious purposes, for the carriage of pilgrims to Mecca. From Medina, which is the terminus, pilgrims travel by camel caravan to Mecca, the journey taking ten days. The money for the construction of the line was subscribed by Moslems all over the world, and no Christians or people of other than the "true faith" were ever allowed to travel farther south upon it than Maan, some distance below Amman.

On the first day of this expedition the New Zealanders left the Jordan Valley, the Turks being driven from their positions in the foothills comparatively easily. The wild flowers growing in the defiles and gullies traversed by the long string of horsemen were very beautiful. Scarlet anemones and a host of other blooms made a riot of colour most pleasing to the eye after the comparative barrenness of the Jordan flats.

Climbing by devious routes through the hills, mostly in single file, the Brigade bivouacked that night high up in the misty tops of Gilead. Moving on next day, a bitterly cold, wet morning, after a wet night, our men travelled in single file across rocky hillsides and up a deep gully, crossing and recrossing a mountain torrent, until the Circassian village of Ain Es Sir was reached. This was occupied without resistance, about fifty Turkish line of communication troops being taken prisoner.

The Circassians were surly-looking scoundrels, most of them wearing the Arab head-dress, a flowing cloth, secured by a woollen or alpaca rope passing twice round the crown of the head. Their clothes were semi-European, dirty coats or waistcoats being worn with heavy breeches baggy above the knee and tapering to the ankle. As they moved furtively about they concealed the lower parts of their faces with the loose folds of their head-cloths, and their eyes shot hostile glances at the invading troops, for their sympathies were known to be Turkish. Our men were to have further experience of this hostility later, at the cost of valuable lives.

The tableland which lies beyond the Mountains of Gilead having been reached, the Brigade was next swung round to the right flank of the attack, coming into action against the Turks near Kissir station, on the railway line. Hundreds of armed Arabs were encountered in this locality, all armed to the teeth, nominally on the British side, but, although they hated the Turks, actually out for whatever loot they could get from either side.

They were treacherous but picturesque ruffians, nearly all carrying modern high velocity rifles, one or two bandoliers, and a profusion of wicked looking knives. It was amusing to see how quickly, once the Turks were driven off part of the railway line, these rascals set to work to chop down the enemy's telegraph posts for firewood, which they carted away on horses or donkeys.

These Arabs were not risking their skins unnecessarily, but at Kissir a charge by mounted Arabs was witnessed which shed a ray of humour on the grim business of fighting, and would have delighted the heart of a cinematograph operator. Some New Zealanders attacked a small force of Turks who were holding the station buildings, and after a short fire fight successfully beat down the enemy opposition, and prepared to surround them as prisoners.

A number of Arab horsemen, who had been lying low in some safe spot nearby, seeing the Turks were beaten, galloped out, and, firing their rifles in the air and emitting blood-curdling yells, descended on the hapless Turks like a whirlwind. Dragging their victims out, they quickly stripped them of their possessions, our men arriving just in time to prevent the Arabs murdering them all, from which purpose they took considerable dissuasion. The Turks, needless to say, were in the condition popularly known as "having the wind up" until their fate was settled, and they were escorted to the rear by British soldiers.

The weather was bitterly cold and wet, the

greatest difficulty being experienced in getting supplies up to advanced troops such as the New Zealand Brigade, who on more than one occasion were without rations or horsefeed. Everything had to be packed on camels over wet, slippery tracks and rocks, up steep hills, where these animals travelled very slowly as they slithered and slid in all directions.

The Egyptian natives of the Camel Transport Corps stuck to their work well, shivering in their blue cotton clothes with a ground sheet or sack thrown over their shoulders. So severe was the weather on this expedition that a number of men in the British force died of exposure.

For a day or two our men held positions in the hills on the extreme right, near Kissir, with the Imperial Camel Corps, where they came under heavy shell-fire. During this time, from a neighbouring hill, they witnessed a gallant but unsuccessful attempt by some of the Camel Corps to storm a strong Turkish position, in which they were beaten off with very heavy loss. The enemy held the top of a hill, apparently not in great strength. On the attack being developed, however, Turks appeared in swarms from over the crest, and poured a devastating fire into the small force attempting the assault; this forced them back to some slight cover half way up the hill, where they lay until it was possible for the remnant to withdraw at night.

The Turks made a practice of shelling concealed hollows which might be made use of as lines of approach, and at this stage of the operations secured a direct hit which justified the expenditure of so much artillery ammunition in this way. A squadron of the Auckland Regiment was moving up to a position in the rocks by way of a depression that the enemy could not possibly observe, when one of these chance shells burst fairly on the mounted column. The result of its explosion was a bloody sight, seven men and eight horses being put out of action.

As the operations proceeded, the New Zealand Brigade was ordered, as part of a combined attack on the town of Amman from three sides, to take a big dome-shaped hill which was one of the dominating features of the landscape, and was heavily held by the enemy.

Concentrating in a gully one cold morning at two a.m., the New Zealanders advanced in one long line towards the Turkish positions fifteen hundred yards away. The different units in the line keeping touch in the dark wonderfully well, they got to within a short distance of the Turkish sangars before they were observed, when a tornado of rifle and machine-gun fire opened on them, the roar of musketry and the fatal chatter of machine-guns making night hideous with their din.

Fortunately, a great deal of this fire went high, and the advance culminated in a determined bayonet charge and savage hand to hand fighting in which the Turkish resistance was soon overcome.

During this assault in the dark one of our signallers had a strange experience. He was following up one of the attacking units, laying a field telephone wire as he went. In the preoccupation of doing this he lost touch, and went up the wrong hill. Before he realized what had happened, he was confronted by some Turks in a trench only a few yards before him. To run would have been useless, so, in the darkness, inarticulately muttering what few words of Arabic he could remember, he succeeded in getting into the trench beside them unrecognized as an enemy.

Ultimately his slouch hat was his undoing, for, one of the Turks having distinguished it in the darkness, they fell upon him and would have killed him but for the intervention of a Turkish officer. This trench had been missed in the main assault, but shortly some Wellington men charged it with a yell—most of the Turks bolted, but the signaller fell upon the officer and took him prisoner, being nearly bayoneted by another New Zealander as he grappled with the Turk in the bottom of the trench. The captor thus became the captured, and at once handed over a fine pair of glasses to the New Zealander. The Turkish officer seemed to regard his one-time prisoner as his special protector under changed conditions, for he followed him about closely until eventually handed over to an escort and taken to the rear.

Our men now held the top of the hill, but as

the chilly wet dawn broke the Turks commenced to shell the position very heavily, having it ranged to a yard.

The gradually growing light revealed an isolated Turkish trench on the left flank which enfiladed the New Zealanders, this post having been missed in the dark. The Turks in it made things very lively for our men on the left of the line till they found cover in a depression on top of a rocky knob. Then a hot fire fight raged between the two small groups, at a range of about three hundred yards. Eventually the accuracy of the New Zealanders' Hotchkiss and machine-gun fire determined the issue, when the Turks hoisted four white flags, and were soon after brought in as prisoners.

Throughout the day the New Zealanders lay on the main hill top, holding on grimly under incessant heavy shell-fire, and successfully beating off two determined counter attacks made by the enemy. It was very cold, and rations were exhausted. The ground was of too rocky a nature to make trenches possible, the only shelter our men had being what little they could get behind flat rocks or low stone sangars, so that the casualties from accurately burst shrapnel were heavy. The New Zealand Brigade had no artillery support, our guns being unable to get up the rocky narrow mountain tracks over which the mounted riflemen had passed, so that throughout the day the hard-won position was grimly held under the fire of about fifteen

A typical East of Jordan cut-throat.

Jerusalem from the Mount of Olives.

A leave party approaching the Mosque of Omar, Jerusalem.

The Monastery built into the face of the "Mount of Temptation," above Jericho.

Turkish guns. The horses had a hard time, having to remain saddled almost constantly for days, and getting little to eat beyond what grazing could be had under cover close to our positions. As they held the hill, our men could get occasional glimpses of the engagement on the country below them, where could be seen the white puffs indicating shrapnel bursts and moving dots they knew to be men—sometimes stopping suddenly to move no more.

Modern battle, with the importance of concealment so necessary in every phase, is uninspiring to watch, as so little is visible to the eye. The spectacular incidents such as a bayonet charge usually occur at night or in the indistinct half light of dawn. The features which impress themselves most strongly on one's senses are the noises, the horrible sights, and smells. The varied noises and crashing of explosives impress themselves strongly on heightened sensibilities. Under shell-fire, if it is not too intense to smother individual reports in a shattering roar, one hears the "wumph" of the enemy gun in the distance, followed by the whine of the approaching shell. This is intensified into a shrieking hiss as it passes close overhead and bursts with a roar and cloud of smoke nearby. If a shrapnel shell, the smoke will be white, and the report will be followed by a vicious whirring as the shrapnel bullets find their marks and the heavy shell-case and nosecap land with a thud or a squelch. If the enemy is using high explosive shells fired from a high velocity gun, the muffled boom of the gun will be followed immediately by a deafening crash, as the shell bursts overhead in a cloud of black smoke and drives its death-dealing jagged fragments to the ground beneath. Rifle fire is heard rising and falling with a popping and crackling noise, which grows to a sustained roar in the heat of an engagement; the bullets coming over with a swishing hiss or a thud when one finds a billet; while the deadly machine-gun contributes its quota to the inferno in a staccato "prp-rp-rp-rp-rp-rp" as one of the main items in the chorus of death.

Other units participating in the attack failed to reach their objective, so that as a concerted operation the attack on Amman failed, and at nightfall our Brigade was ordered to withdraw as soon as the wounded could be got out. Field ambulances could not get within miles of the area, so that the wounded had to be carried out on camels and tied to horses, the agony of which was fatal to several.

Retiring some miles that night, the New Zealanders the following night took up an outpost line to cover the withdrawal of a big force of infantry and camels. Everyone was chilled to the bone, and quite expecting an attack from a superior force of Turks. Fortunately this did not eventuate, and in the early hours of the morning, before daylight, the Brigade withdrew, acting still as rearguard.

The retiring force passed through the Circassian village of Ain Es Sir, and then down a narrow defile. As the last squadron of the rearguard left this place, the inhabitants, who were armed, turned on our men, and treacherously shot three officers and several men. The rearguard at once replied, but, owing to the pressure from the Turks reported as coming on, it was not possible to deal as effectively with the village as our men would like to have done. The Brigade eventually reached the Jordan, and went into bivouac near Jericho.

This expedition, perhaps the most severe experience the Brigade had in the whole of the Campaign, was referred to in the press as a "successful raid." Apart from casualties, the only loss inflicted on the enemy was a temporary dislocation of his railway traffic south of Amman. There our forces had blown up several small culverts and part of the line, but the damage done was quickly repaired by the Turks, who had trains running over the section soon after the British withdrawal. A ten-arched stone railway viaduct, the destruction of which would have been the only effective means of cutting the line, was not reached, the damage done to the enemy being hardly justified by the heavy British casualties suffered. It was therefore somewhat surprising to those who had taken part in the operations to find them described as a success, and as on more than one occasion, made the press reports, in the light of knowledge of the truth, seem more or less facetious.

Chapter XIV.

At Jericho the New Zealanders were in reserve to the troops holding the Ghoraniyeh bridgehead on the river, "standing to" every morning. They were in addition supplying troops to hold other minor fords and crossings of the Jordan where the enemy might have attempted to force a crossing. Shortly after the return from the disastrous Amman raid, they were subjected to a bombing attack by seven Turkish aeroplanes, which is worth mention, as on this occasion the bombs used were of Allied manufacture. One light bomb knocked out eighteen horses and wounded five men. One of the bombs dropped was a "dud," and was identified as one that had been sent to Russia amongst munitions from the Allies, taken by the Germans on the Russian collapse, and sent down to Turkey. Our men were quite convinced of the efficiency of such munitions from this experience.

While in this bivouac many men took the opportunity of viewing the Dead Sea, which was only a few miles away, at close quarters. It was a common practice to ride down, when things were quiet, to Rujm El Bahr, at the northern end of the Dead Sea, where the

Jordan River runs into it. There they bathed themselves and horses. The water is extremely salt and buoyant, and many of the horses, which had bathed before in fresh water or the Mediterranean Sea, were obviously perplexed at floating so high out of the water.

This inland sea is about forty-seven miles in length, its greatest breadth being about ten miles, steep mountain country sloping down to the water on each side. The water contains about twenty-five per cent. of mineral salts, and it is said that an egg will float in it with a third of its volume above the surface. It has been calculated that six and a half million tons of water fall into the Dead Sea daily from various streams, the whole of which huge quantity must be carried off by evaporation, as it has no outlet. This helps to give some idea of the humid heat of the atmosphere in these parts. The surface of the sea lies 1,290 feet below the sea-level of the Mediterranean.

Besides Jericho, and Rujm El Bahr, where are a few decrepit buildings (much in request as firewood) there are no other villages in the Jordan in this locality. The only other human habitations are the rough shelters of the wandering Bedouins and several monasteries.

Of these buildings, one is situated near the river in the direction of the Dead Sea, while another is close to the river by one of the fords, and was for some time used by the New Zealanders as a post for observing enemy movements on the far bank of the river. Another is to be found built into the rock high up on the face of the Mount of Temptation, overlooking Jericho and the Valley.

A prickly scrub abounds in the Jordan Valley, from the formidable thorns of which Christ's crown is said to have been made. Near Jericho is found a woody scrub three or four feet in height, with broad leaves woolly on the under side. The fruit, not unlike an apple, is often called the Apple of Sodom. Of animal life, storks are to be seen, and big vultures, which perch on the chalky bluffs overlooking the river, like so many grim sentinels. Our men occasionally saw wild pigs, while the river itself contains many fish, and its marshy borders abound with frogs and other small fry. Most of the New Zealanders bathed in the Jordan at one time or another during the many months they were in the Valley. It is doubtful, however, if their spiritual refreshment, or whatever benefit the pilgrims imagine they derive from the dip, was so great as their physical benefit during this campaign in which a good bath was such a luxury.

It has been mentioned that the New Zealanders while bivouacked near Jericho were called on to supply troops for holding various posts on the river, and as this was typical of what they were continually required to do when in bivouac, it will not be amiss to follow in detail the doings of a troop sent out on post for a twenty-four hours' tour of duty.

Probably getting two or three hours' notice, the troop detailed for duty would parade mounted, carrying a full supply of ammunition and rations, at Regimental Headquarters. Here the troop-leader would receive his orders. Moving off, they would march perhaps eight or nine miles, often in single file, crossing the deep gullies with which the country is intersected near the river. The horses would be watered en route if an opportunity occurred, and they would probably arrive to relieve the other troop on their post at 6 p.m., or as darkness fell.

Here the relieved troop would hand over to their successors any information likely to be of use as to enemy patrols, posts, or ranges to important points, and then gladly set out on their march back to camp. The officer or sergeant in charge of the troop would then look over the ground and decide on the best spot for the horses, under cover from view and fire. The disposition of the troop had then to be seen to, this probably involving the selection of a place for a listening post to be occupied during the night, in front of the general position. The site allowing for the best use of the Hotchkiss automatic rifle, with which each troop was equipped, would also have to be chosen.

These matters attended to, sentries would be posted, and, if a hollow screened from observation could be found, the men would boil up their little billies and make a rough repast while the horses were fed. On work of this kind the horses always remained saddled, and were usually "linked"—that is, tied together by their headropes, so that in an emergency they could quickly be got out. In addition to sentries, horse-pickets would be required to watch the horses, so that few of the troop would get much sleep.

Each troop in the New Zealand Brigade carried a Hotchkiss automatic rifle, and had a section of four men trained in its use. On troop adventures such as the one under description, where the troop-leader often wished he had a hundred men instead of twenty-five or less, it was an invaluable weapon. The gun is air-cooled, can fire as fast as a machine-gun, but has the advantage of a single-shot adjustment, which will often enable the man behind the gun to get the exact range by single shots indistinguishable from rifle fire, and then to pour in a burst of deadly automatic fire. The gun will not stand continued use as an automatic without overheating, but despite this it is a most useful weapon, light enough to be carried by one man dismounted. On trek, or going into action, a pack-horse in each troop carried the Hotchkiss rifle, spare barrel, and several panniers of ammunition, while a reserve of ammunition was carried by another pack-horse for each two troops. The ammunition was fed into the gun in metal strips, each containing thirty rounds.

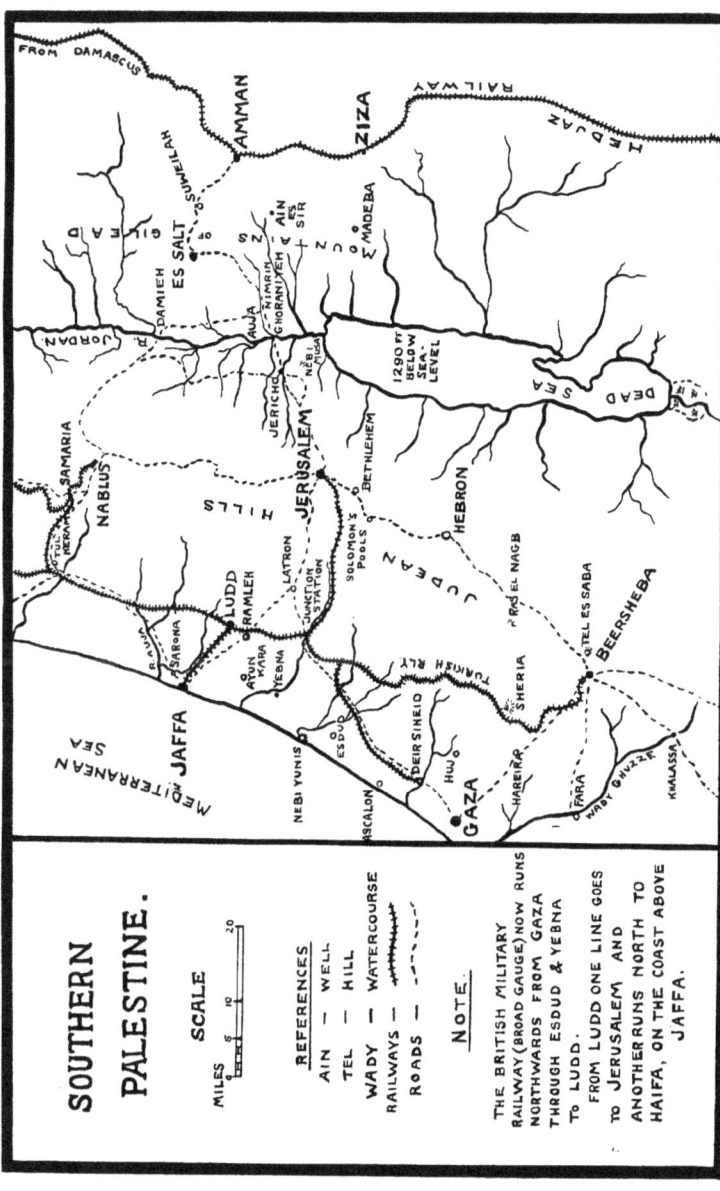

On post, the Hotchkiss would always be placed where it could do the most damage, and all night a man would be lying near it, with the first strip inserted in the breach, ready to spit out death at a moment's notice.

The night of our troop on post might pass uneventfully — on the other hand, rifle fire in front, and the ricochetting of bullets overhead, might give all hands an anxious time as they peered into the darkness in the hope of information from their listening post in front. Perhaps the firing would die down, and silence reign once more, except for the occasional restless movements of the horses, the rolling of a dislodged clod down a hillside, or the weird baying of jackals. Thus the night might pass, or a sinister stillness might suddenly be broken by a crash of rifle fire near at hand, and the hurried tumbling in of panting men from the listening post, with information of the direction of an enemy attack. Then, if the enemy appeared to be in greatly superior numbers from their rifle flashes and vaguely-seen dim forms, each man would know a stern fight was before him. For if the orders were to hold the position, it must be some hours before the troop could be reinforced from the Regiment, miles away. So would the little band hang on in a grim defence, while the bullets hissed over them or went "phut" into the ground nearby, and the deadly stammer of the Hotchkiss rose through the din in a stuttering roar.

Assuming that our troop weathers the hours of darkness with nothing more eventful occurring than a few stray shots, and perhaps the sounds of an enemy patrol moving somewhere in front, the eerie hour of dawn would see a few tired figures creeping in, as the men of the listening post return to their troop ready for what the day may bring forth. If things are quiet, this is the time of relaxation after a more or less sleepless night, for now one sentry, with glasses, is all that need be on watch, and the remainder set about feeding themselves and horses somewhere under cover.

The day may give opportunities of "potting" at Turks if they show themselves in range, or the troop may see enemy aeroplanes come over to reconnoitre the British bivouacs for signs of any hostile movements, and interestedly watch them running the gauntlet as the white puffs of shrapnel or black splotches of high explosive anti-aircraft shells burst around them thousands of feet up in the air. This interest, however, may be tempered with a certain amount of bad language from the troop if the enemy planes happen to be about half way between them and the British anti-aircraft guns. For the air will presently fill with a slowly growing musical note as "spare parts" in the form of shrapnel, shell fragments, and nosecaps, begin to fall, with a whirring noise, from the sky to the ground all around them; the spent parts of the exploded shells fired at the enemy airmen, still with a sufficient momentum in falling to knock a man out.

The Turk may have located this post and decided to shell it, when soon after it is light there will be a muffled roar in the distance, a whine that quickly grows to a hissing shriek, and with a shocking crash in the stillness a shell bursts near at hand. Every man gets behind whatever cover is available, and anxious eyes watch the horses in the hope that they will not be hit. A sigh of relief goes round as the enemy shots go wider and wider with each successive shell, apparently searching the ground for the exact location of the post. Then perhaps the shell-fire will cease, "Jacko," as our men call the Turk, having decided that the expenditure of more ammunition on such an unsatisfactory target is not worth while.

Later in the day the post may be visited by an artillery officer keen to hear of any new targets that our men may have located before them on enemy ground, or perhaps even a colonel or general may appear, wishing to acquaint himself with all the features of the front he is responsible for.

So the day draws to a close, until, as the dust cloud heralding the arrival of the relieving troop appears in the distance, the order is given "Saddle Up!" (it being usual to off-saddle by day), and then "Get Ready to Move!" Then after a brief account of occurrences has been handed over from one troop to another, our troop sets out on its march back to the Regimental bivouac.

Watering the horses en route they arrive smothered in dust, but in good humour, and quickly have the horses once more tied on the lines and themselves settled down into the usual routine. Possibly one of the far too few mails from home has arrived, and, with their mates, they are soon absorbed in welcome letters and illustrated papers, until duty claims them for some necessary work once more.

Chapter XV.

After the first unsuccessful attempt by the British to take Amman, the usual routine continued for some time in the Valley, and then the New Zealanders were concerned in a second attempt on the same objective, which took place at the end of April. It was usual, later, to refer to this as the "second Amman stunt," although the primary objective was Es Salt. But no doubt the successful occupation of Es Salt would have been but a step towards the attacking of Amman, the point on the Hedjaz railway through which came all enemy supplies.

In these operations the Brigade was first thrown in on the right flank of the attack on the Turkish positions in the foothills of Gilead. This was to draw Turkish fire from the British infantry, who were in a tight corner. Then they were moved across to the other flank, to the Umm Shert ford of the Jordan, where their task was to cover the retirement of some Australian units. These Australians had in a brilliant manoeuvre successfully reached Es Salt, high up in the hills, but owing to the failure of the attack elsewhere, notably at Shunet Nimrin, a naturally strong position heavily held by the Turks further south in the foothills, had to be withdrawn. This they just managed to do with the assistance of the New Zealand Brigade.

The New Zealanders remained in the Jordan Valley throughout the summer of 1918, with the exception of two spells of barely a fortnight each spent in the hills near Bethlehem. One of these breaks occurred in the beginning of June, the other in August.

On both occasions the Brigade trekked up the winding white road, through the Hills of Judea, which runs between Jericho and Jerusalem. Stopping one night at Talat Ed Dum, a dry, dusty bivouac, they passed next day through Bethany, and, skirting the walls of the Holy City, travelled through modern Jerusalem, and so out along the Hebron road to the bivouac site.

It was while in these bivouacs, having brief spells from the Jordan Valley, that most of our men got the opportunity of seeing Jerusalem. Leave parties from each regiment would ride in the eight or nine miles to the Holy City in the morning, spend the day sight-seeing, and return in the evening. Of the many photographs sent back to New Zealand by men of the Mounted Brigade, most were of historical spots such as seen round about Jerusalem, and seldom of the deadly monotonous places where their work kept them for the greater part of their time. From this some people seemed to derive the impression that the Mounted Riflemen were having some sort of a "Cook's tour." This was far from being the case, as it was only during infrequent breaks, such as these, in the long months of unending work and discomfort, that the men got the opportunity of seeing these places. Even when nominally "resting" like this, a trooper's time was never his own—horse-pickets had to do their turn every night just the same, guards had to be supplied, while pumping parties for watering the horses, and endless other working parties were called for.

While "spelling" near Bethlehem, our men watered their horses twice daily at the ancient "Pools of Solomon"—great oblong cisterns of stone, some hundreds of feet long, still in good repair. The pumps were worked by the pumping parties on a ledge in one of the cisterns, the water being delivered into the canvas troughs above, where the horses could be brought in. These hand-pumps and canvas troughs were carried everywhere with the Brigade, and where water was available could be quickly erected and brought into operation. The writer made an incautious inquiry as to the historical origin of these huge, well-built reservoirs — a dusty individual, looking up from between the two horses he was watering, volunteered the information that Solomon built them for bathing his many wives—but the informant was under suspicion as a humorist.

While in these parts, the New Zealanders saw the local crop of barley being gathered in, and the grain being winnowed. The whole process of agriculture as practised by the natives of the Holy Land is most primitive, their methods being still the same as were used in the time of Christ. Only in some of the German and Jewish agricultural colonies will modern implements and ways of working be seen. Ploughing and sowing is done at the beginning of the rainy season, about November, or later. The type of plough in general use by the natives is very crude, consisting merely of an upright stick, having a metal-shod toe like a double edged share; to the upright stick, which usually has a cross-piece at the top for a handle, is attached another piece of wood projecting forwards, to which the team is yoked. With this implement the tiller of the soil goes up and down his little plot of land, breaking it into small furrows but a few inches deep. Teams of all varieties are in use, from that of two oxen, to a single camel, the quaintest combinations being seen; often an ox and a donkey—sometimes a camel and an ox.

At harvest-time, the crop is cut, usually by the women, with sickles, and gathered into sheaves. These sheaves are taken into the threshing-floor, being carried by camels, donkeys, and the womenfolk. For in Palestine, the native women are but the chattels of their lords and masters, and are expected to do a big part of the work that supports the family. On the threshing-floor, the oxen, roped together

Germans captured in the Jordan escorted as prisoners past the historic walls of Jerusalem, through which years before their Kaiser had entered in state.

New Zealanders descending to the Jordan at Damieh after driving the Turks from their positions defending the crossing.

New Zealanders passing through the mountain town of Es Salt the morning after its capture.

four or five abreast, tread out the corn, which is spread out like the bottom of a sheaf-stack. A couple of youngsters will usually be seen superintending them, one forking the corn into the path of the animals as the other drives them monotonously round and round. Often the family donkey will be seen attached to one flank of the slow moving team, "doing his bit." When the corn has been well trodden, and is crushed into chaff with the grain amongst it, it is winnowed. This is done on a breezy day by natives armed with broad wooden forks. With these tools they throw a mass of the crushed corn into the air—the wind blows the chaff and dust to one side, and the grain falls at their feet. The women finally go through the grain with a riddle, to clean it, when it is ready to be sold or made into flour for their own use.

Bethlehem, picturesquely set in the surrounding country, was visited by many New Zealanders, the historical Church of the Nativity being viewed with interest.

The road into Jerusalem runs northwards along the Judean hilltops, the ride in from Bethlehem being a pretty one.

Chapter XVI.

As people at home may be interested to hear of what our men saw in the Holy City during the brief opportunities afforded them, some description of the Jerusalem of to-day may not be out of place.

The town is situated 2,500 feet above sea-level, on the southern part of a badly watered and somewhat sterile plateau of limestone, which is connected towards the north with the main range of the mountains of Palestine, and surrounded on all other sides by ravines. The ground occupied by the town is somewhat undulating. The town proper, *i.e.*, the Holy City, is enclosed by a wall nearly forty feet high, forming an irregular quadrangle about two and a half miles in circumference; it has eight gates, one of which has been walled up for centuries. The streets of the old town are ill-paved and crooked, many of them being blind alleys, and are excessively dirty after rain. Some of them are vaulted over into evil-smelling passages. The modern part of the city, which is estimated to contain about half the population, is built outside the city walls, and the suburbs contain many fine buildings well executed in stone. The pre-war population of Jerusalem was estimated at 70,000, of which 10,000 were Moslems, 45,000 Jews, and 15,000 Christians. Great numbers of the Jews subsist on the charity of their European brethren, from whom they receive a regular allowance, and for whom they pray at the Holy places.

When the British captured Jerusalem it was in an indescribably filthy condition, with a nearly starving population. There was no proper water supply, the inhabitants being dependent on such rainwater as could be collected in wells and cisterns, which often collected as much drainage as anything else. This condition of things the British authorities quickly remedied; the town was subjected to a thorough cleaning-up process, and British army engineers piped in a supply of good water soon afterwards. This latter achievement was a testimony to British thoroughness, when it is remembered that it was done during the progress of a big campaign, when the limited railway accommodation was strained to the utmost for the carriage of necessary supplies.

Ludd, within a few miles of Jaffa and the coast, was for some time the railhead for the British broad-gauge railway which had followed the troops across Sinai and Southern Palestine. From there, supplies were brought to Jerusalem on captured rolling stock on the Turkish line. This narrow gauge line was altered, without interference with the traffic, by widening cuttings and strengthening embankments, and by laying the broad-gauge line astride the narrow gauge; so that during 1918 the British had rolling stock off English railways running into Jerusalem station.

It is now possible to go from Cairo to Jerusalem in one railway carriage, over the Suez Canal by the new bridge at Kantara, and so finally up the steep grades approaching Jerusalem, which tax the engines to the utmost of their panting strength.

The holy places in the ancient city were rigidly guarded by the British from any form of desecration, and sentries with fixed bayonets stood on guard at all the gates through which the traffic passed. The places of worship of Moslems, such as the Mosque of Omar, were guarded by Indian sentries of that faith, and everything was done to give the oppressed people confidence in British administration.

The New Zealanders usually entered the Holy City in charge of an officer, by the Kaiser's entrance, adjoining the Jaffa Gate, passes showing their authority for entrance having to be produced to the sentries. The Jaffa Gate, through which General Allenby made his triumphal entry into the Holy City on foot, is quite an insignificant archway in the massive walls. The main stream of traffic passes through the big breach in the wall, which was made some years ago, in 1898, for the Kaiser's entry into the city, on the occasion of his theatrical tour of the Holy Land. The wall on the left of the opening, as the sightseer enters, is surmounted by a clock-tower built in memory of the event, which is quite out of harmony with its surroundings, but evidently fulfilled the requirements of a fitting memorial to the Teutonic mind.

Inside the walls, the first place visited was usually the Church of the Holy Sepulchre, built over the site of Calvary. Just inside the door is seen the "Stone of Unction," on which the body of Christ is said to have been anointed by Nicodemus. The atmosphere of the Church is heavy, and invaded with the mysterious odour of incense.

The centre of interest is the Holy Tomb, an ornate structure housing it under the big dome of the Church. The interior of the dome is sadly out of repair, the decoration having in many places peeled away. The edifice enclosing the Tomb is to the Western mind somewhat over-decorated. The interior is divided into two, a small ante-chamber giving on to the tiny Chapel of the Holy Sepulchre, which is only six and a half feet long and six feet wide. The Tomb lies on the right as one enters, covered with marble slabs, the topmost one of which is cracked across the middle. From the roof of the tiny Chapel depend forty-three brass lamps of the most beautiful workmanship. A priest of the Church stands by constantly on vigil.

As instancing the trickery and hypocrisy practised here, on a spot which should be one of the most hallowed to Christians, may be mentioned a rite performed annually. Things of this nature did much to disillusion our men as to the "holiness" of the present-day Jerusalem. An observer will notice a circular aperture in the side of the structure housing the Tomb. On enquiry, he will be told that this is the orifice from which, at the Easter Festival, issues the "Holy Fire." At this ceremony great numbers of pilgrims gather round the Tomb, and strive to light their tapers from the flame. Doubtless these people, many of them sincere, but also ignorant and credulous, are much impressed by the manifestation of the so-called "miracle" which may be trusted to result in the acquisition of many shekels by someone.

Truly Jerusalem, which might be expected to be one of the most godly cities, is, owing to the fanaticism and jealous exclusiveness of the numerous religious communities, one of the most material places on earth. An excess of the outward forms and ceremonial of religion seems to have stifled the true spirit of it which Christ strove to impart in these surroundings.

Climbing some steep and slippery steps, one stands on the site of Calvary, where are the altars of the various churches of the Christian Faith, side by side, the subdued candle-light glittering on the many offerings of gold ornaments and precious stones sent from all over the world. Descending again, one may get a view of the rock from underneath, and see the crack where the stone was split on the day of the Crucifixion.

From the Church of the Holy Sepulchre one may walk down the narrow stone-paved Via Dolorosa, up which Christ made his painful way to Calvary bearing the Cross, pausing at the various "stations" where He halted in His progress. At one of these stations may be seen the Church of Ecce Homo, a substantial modern building, enclosing, at the altar, part of the original stonework which witnessed the passing of Christ. This is said to mark the spot where Pilate uttered the words, "Behold the Man!"

A scene of interest is the Jews' "Wailing Place," where the Jews of the town pour out their prayers and lamentations against a towering wall of huge blocks of stone. The women may be seen kissing the wall and weeping, while the men will often stay for hours reading from their well-thumbed Hebrew prayer-books.

One may then enter the precincts of the ancient Temple of Solomon, on which now stands the Mosque of Omar, or Temple of the Rock, and the Mosque of El Aksa. These are both fine buildings, and the centre of Moslem worship in Jerusalem. The Mosque of Omar is particularly imposing, standing in the middle of a large stone-paved area with no other buildings near it. The building is octagonal in design, the walls, which are a mass of beautiful mosaics, being surmounted by a huge dome, on top of which is the crescent. Outside the door all footgear must be removed — when many troops were viewing the sights of Jerusalem, the pavement near the door of the Mosque presented rather a comical aspect with an assorted heap of boots, leggings, and spurs. On entering, the dome is seen to be magnificent in its interior decoration, while the windows, all of different design, shed a soft light on to the rich carpets underfoot. In the centre, underneath the dome, is the huge red rock from which the place takes its name, the ancient sacrificial stone of old. The general effect of the Mosque of Omar is one of artistic grandeur, which impresses itself on one in contrast to the comparative tawdriness of the Christian Church built over Calvary.

The Mosque of El Aksa is interesting, but in no way striking, being rather dwarfed by the splendid edifice adjoining it. In front of each building will be seen an Indian sentry with fixed bayonet — symbols of the power of Empire which brings a native of alien faith from his own country, and puts him to guard the places of his worship in another land; a land, moreover, wrested from an enemy of the same religious faith as himself.

One may then walk across the remainder of the enclosed space on which once stood Solomon's Temple, and, passing the closed " Golden Gates " in the city wall, (which prophecy says are to open one day for the

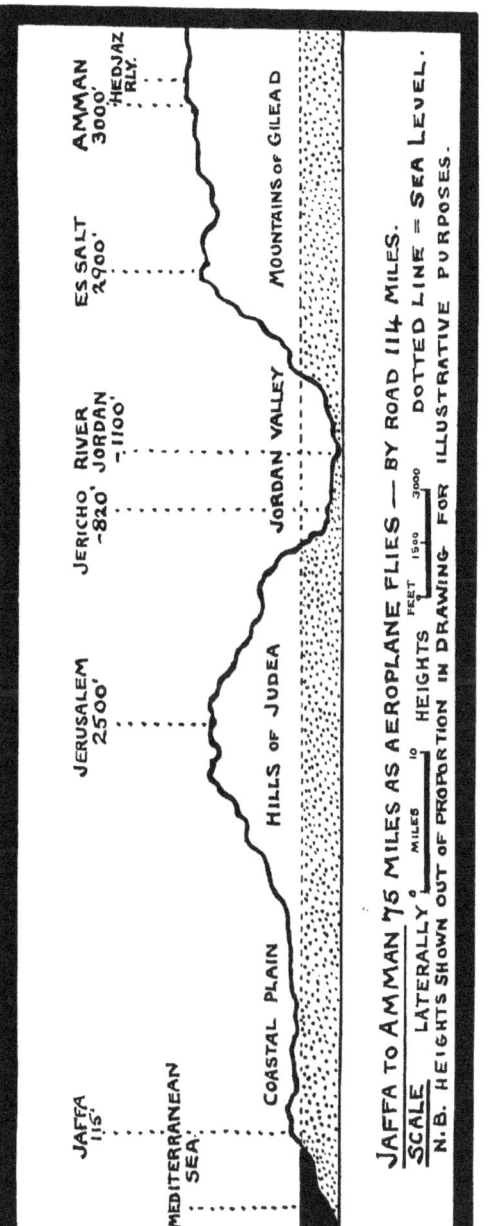

passage of a conqueror) come to St. Stephen's Gate. Passing through the small archway, probably in company with an Arab and his donkey going out to the Jericho road, one sees, immediately below, the Valley of Kidron, or Valley of Jehosophat. On the far side of this valley, where it commences to slope up towards the Mount of Olives, is seen the Garden of Gethsemane, enclosed from the dusty road on two sides of it by a high stone wall.

Above it rises the Mount of Olives, the trees from which it takes its name scattered over it but sparsely. Running along the bottom of the valley, and disappearing to the right up and over the shoulder of the Mount of Olives, is the dusty white road to Jericho. Shortly after it disappears from sight, the road passes through the village of Bethany, which was such a favourite resort of Our Lord. This village now consists of only about forty ramshackle hovels, rather picturesquely situated amongst fig, olive, and almond trees. This road was the one traversed by the New Zealanders on their journeys between Jericho and Bethlehem.

Of the leave parties that came to Jerusalem, many men would be satisfied after having seen the places mentioned, and would be then only too glad to get a meal and spend the rest of the day taking photographs or buying souvenirs.

Those, however, of an energetic nature, would descend into the valley and see the Garden of

Gethsemane at close quarters, afterwards climbing to the top of the Mount of Olives. From this position of vantage the Dead Sea may be discerned in the distance, its surface 3,900 feet below the level of the beholder. On the top of the hill is a large German Hospice, which was used by the enemy when in occupation of the Holy City. There is also a big Russian building, a nunnery, and one or two churches. There is the Chapel of the Ascension, and the Church of the Lord's Prayer, where Christ is said to have first taught the disciples the Lord's Prayer.

The people of Jerusalem form an interesting study, with their varied types of feature and dress. It strikes an observer that the women of the Jewish race seem to have retained their racial characteristics more strongly than the men, who for the most part appear to be of an indifferent stamp. Many of the younger Jewish women are handsome, with well-marked features.

Outside the Jaffa Gate, where there is most traffic, one may stand awhile and watch the cosmopolitan crowd going by. Arabs pass in their flowing robes, with their distinctive headdress of striped silk or cloth, held in place by its rope-like fastening passing twice round the head; their feet shod in red or brown shoes of native make, made from camel hide. Church dignitaries pass to and fro, both Moslem and Christian, many of the latter wearing quaint, high, cylindrical hats, not unlike "bell toppers" minus the brim, and sombre robes of black. Jews of all types are to be seen, from the ragged individual wearing a battered bowler hat, with a low crown, drawn tight down on to the head, to the obviously well-to-do citizen, attired in modern European dress. Then there are those that wear unkempt curls, side-whiskers and beards, and peculiar flat hats fringed with fur. Every combination of Western and Eastern clothes may be seen, the apparel of some of the passers-by being ludicrously incongruous mixtures, evidently chosen with more regard to opportunity and utility than style.

Through the mixed crowd move the soldiers of the British Empire — the "Tommy" as unconcerned as ever — swarthy Indians, obviously interested in all around them, and soldiers of the Jewish Battalions, easily discernible by their features. An Australian Light Horseman moves along with a jaunty air matching the fluttering plume of feathers in his hat, stopping to exchange a greeting with two New Zealand Mounted Riflemen. These are dusty and suntanned, and easily picked out of the crowd by their distinctive green and khaki hat puggarees, on which one wears the red and white colour-patches of the Auckland Regiment, and the other the black and white check of Canterbury.

A party of natives of the Egyptian Labour Corps straggle by in charge of a lance-corporal, their weird chant and laughing brown faces reminding one of so many big children, and drawing one's attention for a moment as they go. These are followed by two black soldiers of a British West Indies Battalion, one carrying a cane, and both well turned out, with shining buttons, evidently fully alive to their dignity as soldiers of the Empire to which they are proud to belong. Occasionally is seen a woman of Bethlehem, with her peculiar head-dress, which is a white cloth, draped over what might be a tarboosh, on the back of her head.

Thus was Jerusalem as the New Zealanders saw it — rapidly coming back to thriving prosperity, such as had not been known under the Turks, under the benign influence of British administration.

CHAPTER XVII.

After the first spell near Bethlehem, the Brigade returned to the Jordan Valley about the middle of June, 1918.

The following month, on July 14th, at Ain Ed Duc, our line in the Valley north of Jericho, which was held by New Zealanders and Australians, was attacked by the Turks, strongly stiffened with German troops. The attack pierced the line at one point, but the Colonial horsemen quickly got round behind the attacking force and cut them off, eventually surrounding them and taking about seven hundred prisoners. Of these three hundred were Germans, of which Wellington got a number. It was worth notice in this attack that the Turks seemed to have deliberately let the Germans down, as their supporting troops made no serious attempt to follow up the attackers, otherwise our men could never have surrounded them as they did.

With the exception of the second short spell at Bethlehem, in August, our men remained in the Jordan Valley right up till the time of the final operations commencing in September, their work alternating between holding posts in the line, supplying patrols, and acting in support of other units.

Their life in the Valley, from which even the natives migrate in summer, was one of great hardship. The summer heat was intense, ranging up to 120 degrees in the shade. Venomous snakes and scorpions abounded on the ground where they slept, and flies were an ever present evil. The most deadly pest, however, was the malarial mosquito — at night these swarmed around, vicious as miniature tigers in their thirst for human blood. Out of the many hundreds of New Zealanders that were sent to hospital from the Jordan Valley with malaria, many a fine man succumbed to the deadly disease, this being one of the most tragic features of the closing months of the campaign. Many recovered after treatment in hospital, only to suffer a relapse later and to be evacuated again to hospital. Many men were in this way invalided to New Zealand as a result of malaria, with their health badly undermined. The quick absorption of all available reinforcements at this time is thus easily understood.

The Base hospitals being in Cairo, the evacuation of a man with fever occupied many stages, which may be briefly described here, the journey being over three hundred miles.

From his regiment the sick man would be carried on a stretcher to the New Zealand Mounted Field Ambulance, where his case would be diagnosed and a card attached to his clothing giving particulars. He would next be moved to the Anzac Divisional C.C.S. (Casualty

Clearing Station), which would be a little further back in the Valley, handy to the motor road. There he would be placed, with three other stretcher cases, in a motor ambulance, to make the long journey through the hills to Jerusalem, where he would arrive coated in dust. In Jerusalem he would be carried into one of the two big buildings taken over by the British for use as casualty clearing stations. His medical history card would be read and treatment given him, and he might be kept there for a couple of days. Then, if he was considered fit to travel, his stretcher would again make up a load in a motor ambulance, this stage of the journey being to Ludd, near the coast, and on the railway. The journey took from three to four hours over very hilly, dusty roads, being severe on a man with a high temperature. Later, when the broad-gauge line was through to Jerusalem, cases would be sent direct from there by hospital train.

At Ludd the patient would be admitted to another casualty clearing station, where he would perhaps be kept another two days before continuing his journey in a hospital train. This hospital train would land him in a stationary hospital at Gaza, from which, if he was progressing favourably, he would soon be moved by train to a hospital on the sea-shore at El Arish. After another brief stay there, a hospital train would take him on to Kantara. After lying in a hospital at Kantara East for perhaps two or three days, he would be carried in an ambulance across the Suez Canal to Kantara West. From there he would travel the last stage of his journey to a base hospital in Cairo on the Egyptian State Railways.

Unfortunately, the New Zealanders had no hospital of their own in Egypt (since the departure of the other New Zealand troops to France), and so the mounted men were sent to an Imperial Military Hospital, usually the 27th General, in Cairo. It was often wished that a New Zealand hospital for the Mounted Riflemen had been possible, where our men could have had the invaluable care of our own New Zealand nursing sisters. There was a number of New Zealand sisters in the English hospitals, and they will ever be remembered gratefully by the men who were fortunate enough to be nursed by them.

When a man was sufficiently recovered to leave hospital, he was discharged to Aotea Convalescent Home, at Heliopolis, about eight miles from Cairo. This was a convalescent home established for our men by some of the more thoughtful and generous people of New Zealand, and run by a small staff of devoted New Zealand women. These ladies all men of the Mounted Brigade hold in the highest honour for their untiring work in bringing sick and wounded back to health, and giving them a taste of wholesome living after their long spells of roughing it in the field. Their work was often thankless and almost unrecognised by the

Victors and vanquished. Turks killed in the fight for the Bridge at Damieh.

Turkish Prisoners at Amman.

public or Government of New Zealand, but their reward lay in the measure of appreciation in which it was held by the men they cared for. On leaving Aotea, the men were sent back to the Base training camp at Ismailia, on the Suez Canal. There, if they were again fit, they spent a short time in more or less uncongenial drill and camp duties, and were then despatched with a reinforcement draft to rejoin the Brigade. These drafts would contain men rejoining from hospital like this, and men recently arrived from New Zealand going to join the Brigade for the first time—the latter easily distinguishable by their "bloom," which most men lost after a few months as they became thinner and sallow.

The journey "up the line" was very different from that coming down in a hospital train, for a draft usually travelled at night, in practically open trucks. About thirty-five men were packed into each truck, this being a very tight fit with their kits, rifles, forty-eight hours' rations, and loaded bandolier. Morning would find them at Ludd again, after a sleepless night in a bumping, clanking train. There they would have time for a wash and a scratch meal before moving on by train to Jerusalem, where the draft would be accommodated at the Desert Corps camp, a mile or so from the station, for perhaps a night or two. From there they would be despatched in motor-lorries down the hill to Jericho, where led horses would be sent in some miles, from the Brigade bivouac, to meet them and carry them out.

Thus did a man go to hospital, recover, and come back once more, tired but determined, to do his duty in the heat, dust, and other evils of the Jordan.

The soil of the Jordan Valley is of a chalky formation, and under the occupation of troops soon became churned up, until everything lay under a thick blanket of dust, roads and tracks often being nearly a foot deep in it. Any traffic stirred this up into a dense, limey cloud which penetrated everywhere, and stuck grittily to sweat-soaked clothes. Men returning from watering their horses were often weird sights —their scanty clothes would be wet with perspiration, which sometimes dripped from the knees of their riding-breeches. A white coating of dust would enshroud them, through which their faces could be seen as white masks streaked with sweat.

During this period in the Valley, the Turk used to enliven things with spasmodic bursts of long-range shelling. Behind his defences in the hills east of Jordan the enemy possessed a long-range naval pattern six inch gun. With this he used to fire at targets over twelve miles away on the other side of the Valley, on one occasion shelling Jericho with it. The gun thus came to be known as "Jericho Jane." When it was afterwards captured by the British it was found to have a barrel about eighteen feet long, the projectile being very pointed in shape. The shell and charge-case together measured nearly six feet.

Chapter XVIII.

The final operations in Palestine which culminated in the collapse of the Turks, and caused the enemy to sue for an armistice, commenced on the 19th of September, 1918, and in these the New Zealanders took a prominent part.

By means of clever ruses, which included the erection of dummy camps in the Jordan, the use of hundreds of dummy horses, dust clouds created by men and horses detailed for the purpose, and other devices of a like nature, the Turks were led to believe that General Allenby would strike on the Turkish left flank, in the Jordan Valley. For some time previous to the operations our men had an opportunity of exercising their artistic skill in the manufacture of dummy horses. Many thoroughbreds, which must have looked quite awe-inspiring at a distance, owed their racy outlines to a combination of reeds, horse blankets, sandbags, and wire!

A story was told that the British Commander in Chief reserved a suite of rooms in the Jerusalem Hotel for the use of his staff, and had signallers fitting up telephone and other apparatus in the building; this naturally spread in the town as an indication that General Headquarters were going to be established there, on the British right flank, and ultimately got over to the enemy, as it was doubtless intended to do. However this may be, the Turks were completely "bluffed," and consequently massed thousands of troops opposite our positions in the Jordan to meet the expected thrust. Immediately before the operations commenced, the enemy troops on this flank probably outnumbered the British opposing them in the ratio of two or three to one.

When the big offensive was launched on the opposite flank, towards the coast, the troops in the Jordan Valley were called on to act as a pivot for the big turning movement, and hold the force opposing them. This they did, the infantry making some ground northwards in front of the New Zealand Brigade, which was "standing to" in reserve, ready for any emergency.

Then, on the night of September 20th, the Brigade moved out through the British infantry outposts, and by the morning had cleared the ground and taken up positions three miles further on. On this advance, momentarily expecting hot resistance, our men came upon dozens of well-prepared entrenched positions from which the Turks had fled before them. In one place blankets lay on the ground as though their owners had suddenly arisen and fled. It later transpired that only a matter of minutes separated the hurried departure of the Turks from the arrival of our first two mounted patrols at their positions.

On the morning of September 21st, the New Zealand patrols were busy reconnoitring the ground held by the Turks, who evidently had "the wind up," and greeted them with machine-gun fire.

Moving out late that night, the Brigade marched northwards through the darkness, their objective being the Damieh crossing of the Jordan. A main road of vital importance to the enemy ran down to the river at this point from the hills, and crossed to the eastern bank of the river on a pontoon bridge. The Turks had evidently fled soon after nightfall from the positions our patrols had found them in during the day, for no serious resistance was encountered until the leading regiment was astride the road leading down to the bridge from Nablus. There, just before dawn, the advance guard became engaged with the enemy force holding the bridgehead, in the chalky hills near the river.

As dawn broke, the Turks started to shell, and Auckland Regiment pushed into the attack. The other units meanwhile had captured some buildings where the road emerged from the hills into the valley, with a good haul of prisoners. Auckland was reinforced by a squadron of Canterbury and a company of British West Indies infantry, a hot fight ensuing. The Turks finally gave before the onslaught of our troops, and retreated in disorder and under heavy fire across their bridge. As they did so they made great targets for our men, who did good shooting and inflicted heavy casualties, the road leading to the bridge, and the bridge itself, being littered with the corpses of men and horses.

The bridge was captured intact, a total of some five hundred prisoners being secured by the Brigade in the morning's operations. Our casualties were comparatively light in proportion to those of the enemy.

The seizure of this important tactical point by the New Zealanders contributed materially to the success of the operations as a whole, as it cut off the retreat of thousands of retiring Turks west of the Jordan, eventually forcing them to surrender to the British troops who had pushed through further north, by way of the breach made on the other flank.

The morning following the Damieh fight, the New Zealand Brigade assembled on the east bank of the river, and commenced to march on Es Salt, a populous town of some size high up in the Mountains of Gilead. Crossing the few miles of comparatively level country immediately east of the river, our men commenced the long climb up the hills towards their objective. The way led up a narrow mountain track, rocky and steep, the advance being made for the most part on foot, leading the tired horses, a most exhausting march. As they mounted higher and higher, the New Zealanders could see the whole of the lower Jordan Valley spread out before them, lines of dust-clouds indicating the movements of troops below them.

The Turks held good positions on the hill-tops, entrenched and wired, but, fortunately, offered only a half-hearted resistance. By half-past four in the afternoon, the town, nestling in a cup-shaped depression in the hill-tops, had fallen to the New Zealand Brigade, with three hundred and eighty prisoners and three guns.

The advance, in a single day, from country several hundreds of feet below sea-level, to two thousand nine hundred feet above sea-level, where the Brigade bivouacked above Es Salt, brought the men into a very different climate from that of the universally hated Jordan Valley, it being now distinctly cool. This was soon to have a disastrous effect on many men with malaria dormant in their blood, who collapsed rapidly, until at the close of the "stunt" the New Zealand Brigade had lost about sixty per cent. of its strength to hospital.

Probably the feature of Es Salt best appreciated by the New Zealanders was its beautifully cold water, which was eagerly filled into water-bottles from a spring in the town — a great luxury after the constantly warm water of the Valley.

Marching through the quaint main street between the terraced limestone buildings of the town, early next morning, the Brigade moved out in the advance on Amman. As has been indicated before, Amman was a place of importance to the Turks, being the station on the Hedjaz railway through which came all their supplies on this part of the front. The road along which our men travelled bore ample evidence of the work of the Royal Air Force bombing aeroplanes. On the outskirts of Es Salt one heavy bomb had landed on what was probably a market-place, or perhaps a butcher's yard, for dead cattle, sheep, horses, and men lay all round in gory confusion. At intervals the road was littered with the remains of transport waggons, equipment of all sorts, and dead men and horses, which showed how the British 'planes had harassed the retreating Turks.

That night the New Zealanders reached Suweileh, a native village half-way between Es Salt and Amman, where they halted for the night under cover of outposts. From this point, at five o'clock in the evening, a party of four officers and one hundred men set out to try to cut the Turkish railway above Amman. This task they successfully performed, and as this "night stunt" was typical of others carried out at different times by men of the Mounted Brigade, a detailed account written by the Author just after its occurrence, may be appended here.

On the afternoon of September 25th, the advance guard of the New Zealand Mounted Brigade passed through the village of Suweileh, about eight miles beyond Es Salt, and by four p.m. the whole Brigade was drawn up in close formation on some open ground beyond the village.

About a quarter past four, men were called for to form a demolition party to cut the railway above Amman, the Turkish main artery of communication. After a hurried "boil up" and stripping of saddles of gear, the party paraded at Auckland Headquarters shortly after five p.m. It was composed of one hundred picked men and horses, chosen equally from the three Auckland squadrons, commanded by a major, with a subaltern from each squadron. The order was given for stripped saddles, and nothing was carried but the necessary tools — these were just such as could be scraped up in a hurry, and consisted of two picks, two shovels, and four very indifferent spanners. No explosives were available. Every man was fully armed and carrying the maximum of ammunition.

This party penetrated twelve miles into unknown enemy territory at night, took a section out of the Hedjaz line under the noses of the Turkish patrols, and returned next morning without the loss of a man, so an account of the expedition in detail may well be recorded.

The only information as to the route was that a course taken due east would eventually strike the line—the map of the locality was inaccurate, and did not give any idea of the nature of the country, so shortly after leaving Suweileh the column left the road and proceeded to strike across country. A halt was made before it became quite dark, and the column was told off into three parties—one covering party for the left, the demolition party to work on the line, and a covering party for the right, in case the ground near the railway admitted of this system of protection.

The column then moved off silently in the darkness. Protection was afforded by an advanced section of four men and a sergeant under an officer, who kept in front of the column as feelers throughout the journey. It was soon found that the country instead of being easy rolling downs as had been hoped for, resolved itself into difficult going over rocky limestone spurs intersected by deep gullies, making constant reference to the stars and luminous compass a necessity to maintain direction.

The night was inky black, showing up the sparks as the horses tumbled over the rocks— it was a marvel that no horses were disabled. Steadily the column pushed on, now negotiating a boulder-strewn hillside, then dipping into a gully, until in the bottom of a gully a track of sorts was found which travelled roughly in the direction required. This was traversed, and after a mile or two resolved itself into a wide track showing signs of recent traffic. It was not likely that such a good avenue of approach would be neglected, and the alertness of the advanced section was soon justified. The column was halted under a low spur, while three dim figures crept forward on foot to investigate some coughing and other sounds which had been heard in front — were they Bedouins or

Turks? Soon the adventurous three returned, reporting a Turkish post in course of digging in, with open ground in front which precluded the chance of rushing them silently.

As the column was then wedged in a narrow gully, with steep rocky hillsides on either side of them, quite impassable for mounted men, the only thing to do was to turn back and seek another line of approach to the railway which might not be so closely guarded by the enemy. As the element of surprise was necessary to get to the line without giving any warning of its approach, it was essential for the column to endeavour to dodge enemy posts rather than engage them, as even a single rifle shot in the stillness of the night, apart from telephonic communication by which such posts would be linked, would be sufficient to "give the game away."

Therefore the party retraced its way up the gully until it reached a point where, in the light of the newly risen moon, a goat track showed faintly, running up a depression in the spur on the left. This was followed in single file for a considerable distance until the summit was reached, when the long snake-like column once more headed east towards its goal. There was now no track visible, and the best passable way among the rocky gullies had to be picked by the advanced section, which now strung itself out for a considerable distance ahead, the officer and one man picking the way in the lead, with the remainder acting as connecting files at long intervals back to the head of the column.

This course of progress was followed for some time through country over which was scattered a number of Bedouin camps — treacherous as the Bedouins are known to be, it was very necessary to keep well clear of their camps, as none of them would be above trying for a little "baksheesh" from the Turks if they thought it could be obtained by giving warning of our approach. Eventually a cairn of stones on the top of the hill was sighted by the advance party, which was identified as a cairn marked on the map as being on a hill overlooking the railway. The column was drawn up and dismounted in the shadow of a gully below the hill, while the officer commanding the column and the officer on the screen went forward to reconnoitre.

All was silent as the grave as the two pushed up the hill, except for the occasional clink of a horse's hoof against a stone, or the champing of a bit. They reached the summit, and went cautiously over it, when a wave of sound came up to them suddenly from the valley below, and they were the surprised witnesses of a huge Turkish transport column making its way up the road below them to the north, evidently bound for Deraa. The Turks knew that Amman would be threatened soon, how soon they did not realise, and were getting a tremendous mass of material away in time — probably with the idea that the garrison left to defend the town could get away quickly if required by the railway. This, however, did not eventuate — they left Amman by the Es Salt road, as our prisoners, two days later.

Fascinated, the two officers watched the scene in the indistinct haze of moonlight, while a confused medley of sound floated up to them on the night air—the cracking of whips, creaking of wheels, and the shouting of the Turkish drivers. Had these unsuspecting Turks known that two enemy officers were watching them, and a hundred of the dreaded "death riders" were within easy rifle range of them, they would hardly have cracked their whips and shouted to each other with such abandon.

With some difficulty the railway line was at last located as running roughly parallel to the road up which this stream of transport was pouring. Then came the problem of getting down to the line and doing the job, without raising the alarm, when the main road ran within a chain or two of the line. It looked a forlorn hope, but it was decided to get as near to the line as possible and then make use of opportunities. The officers returned to the party, which then worked its way carefully round the shoulder of the hill into a slight hollow in which the horses could not be seen from the road, but from which the line below, about four hundred yards away, could be commanded. Here the column dismounted, and while the men with the tools were sorted out, and the remainder posted where they could bring rifle fire to bear on the line below, an officer with his sergeant and one man climbed gingerly down the hillside and crept along cautiously to find whether the approach to the line could be made by a small party.

On his reporting all clear, a party totalling eight, two officers and six men, just the necessary number to start loosening the bolts, crept down to the line, while a few more with the picks and shovels waited ready to come up when needed. The party on the line had no more than got to work and got the first nuts loosened, when there was a subdued alarm given, and the astonished men looked up to behold a train coming from Amman, round a bend a short distance away. There was no time to get back from the line to cover, and the only cover near the line was composed of two small rocks, about eighteen inches high, not fifteen yards from the rails, behind which the party crawled — four behind each. If they were discovered the game was up, so be sure they lay very, very still in the moonlight, and it was a tense few moments as the big Turkish armoured truck, pushed by an armoured engine, approached. Both truck and engine were crammed full of Turks, singing and talking. Just as they passed the spot, travelling quite slowly, where the eight figures were lying so still, one of them gave a shout. Then the party on the ground thought they were "for it," but the train moved on, and presently went out of sight round another bend. How they passed without seeing the khaki figures on the ground and opening fire on them remains a mystery to this day, and the men concerned will not forget those few moments in a hurry. As soon as the train was out of sight the party set feverishly to work to loosen the nuts where the rails were joined, and the only sounds were the subdued clink of a spanner and the whispered swearing of all at the inadequacy of the tools for the job. A Turk was seen lying not fifty yards on the other side of the line, with a pack-horse standing beside him — the risk of his enquiring the business of the party had to be taken, but as he lay there throughout the operations it was assumed that he was either sick or wounded, or else mistook the party on the line for Turkish railwaymen. Several of the nuts were off when there was another alarm, and all hands lay flat as a Turkish mounted patrol appeared — evidently the railway patrol. One of them halted on his horse barely a chain from the line, on the side of the road, and sat there for fully a minute, so once more the party had to try and make themselves appear a part of the ground they were lying on.

Eventually he moved off, and the work continued, with minor alarms from people on the road, until the joints of the rails were all loosened but one. This stubbornly refused all the efforts of the spanners available, so the men with picks and shovels were brought up, and as quietly as possible loosened the ballast around the iron sleepers, until one end of the section of rails could be prised up. This went on until, by main brute strength, the party lifted the entire section, and wrenched the unbroken joints in such a way as to bend the rail and render a new one essential to repair it.

The breach in the line was not visible for any distance, owing to the way in which it was left, and this fact was no doubt responsible for its wrecking a Turkish supply train en route to Amman later that morning. It was estimated that not less than six hours would be required to repair the break, and this would give all the delay required.

It was by then about three a.m., and the adventurous expedition had only an hour or two of darkness in which to make themselves scarce, so immediately the job was completed all hands got back to the horses, and the column set out on its return journey.

This occupied about three hours, dawn breaking just after the worst of the rocky country had been left behind, and as the party struck the Amman-Suweileh road about four miles from Suweileh. Everyone indulged in a much-longed-for smoke, with the happy consciousness that they had carried out a difficult job successfully. Suweileh was reached at six a.m., just as the Brigade was moving out for the attack on Amman. The demolition party had six hours

A group of Arab Sheikhs on the plateau of Moab.

Leaving the Jordan Valley for the last time. The "Mount of Temptation" in the background.

A column of New Zealanders making arrests in the Nile Delta during the Egyptian rebellion.

in which to feed and sleep, and rejoined the Regiment just in time for the closing acts of the fight for Amman, which resulted in the capture of the town.

A comment on the above is that such a feat could only have been performed by well-mounted troops, pursuing bold tactics, as our men did in all their operations against the Turks. It is also obvious that such an adventure is of the essence of good soldiering — *i.e.*, to cause the maximum of damage to the enemy, whilst suffering the minimum of loss.

Chapter XIX.

After the night's halt at Suweileh, the advance of the Brigade continued on the 25th of September, and the New Zealanders soon deployed and came into action in the hilly country which surrounds Amman. The Turks evidently meant to hold the place, for they put up a stiff resistance, having plenty of artillery and machine-guns. The fight raged throughout the afternoon before the Turks showed any sign of weakening, but our men pressed them hard; as the day waned their defence collapsed, and the New Zealanders were quickly into the town and around the railway station, an Australian Brigade arriving in time to share in the closing phases of the fight.

During the engagement one squadron of New Zealanders galloped into action in troop waves, immediately coming under heavy cross fire from three machine-guns. The squadron dismounted for action, the horseholders galloping back to the cover of a hill with the led horses. One or two men were shot in the saddle, and their uncontrolled horses set the pace for the rest as they galloped madly back, many with blood streaming from flesh wounds in their sides and legs; their arrival behind the hill with manes and tails flying resembled the finish of some classic race, and was a sight worth seeing.

The results of the action were two thousand two hundred prisoners, numbers of guns and machine-guns, and a huge mass of material, the Turkish depôt at the railway station being a litter of supplies of all sorts. It is worth commenting on, that in the four days from Damieh to Amman the New Zealand Brigade had thus taken over three thousand prisoners—twice as many as themselves in number, for the Brigade was below strength from casualties and sickness.

The New Zealanders had the honour of being the leading troops of the force employed, and did all the fighting with the exception of the first advance in the Jordan Valley.

Amman, or, as some maps show it, Rabboth-Ammon, is the Philadelphia of history. Traces of its ancient glory still survive, notably in the big amphitheatre cut out of the side of a hill facing the town, before which still stands a row of handsome pillars. In the town itself portions of old columns may be seen lying by the roadside or doing duty in modern walls. The present day inhabitants are a villainous-looking lot, with a fair sprinkling of the Circassian element in the population.

A mysterious loss in horses occurred here, as many as nine in one troop dying on the lines. Experts could not agree as to the cause of the trouble, some blaming a local poisonous weed, while others thought it originated from some captured grain our men had been giving to their horses.

The country to the south of the town opens out after a while into a comparatively level tableland, with good barley-growing land alongside the railway, more of which the New Zealanders were to see shortly.

With Amman in British hands, our troops were astride the Hedjaz railway, effectually cutting off all the Turks to the south from their base.

A few days later, a force of five thousand Turks, retreating from the Hedjaz, hoisted the white flag at Ziza, a station on the line about fifteen miles south of Amman. An Australian Brigade went out to take their surrender, the New Zealand Brigade going out in support. Marching all night, and arriving at dawn, our men heard rifle-fire and machine-guns chattering ahead of them, and suspected foul play. On drawing near to the scene of the surrender, however, it was seen that both Turks and Australians were firing at the Arabs, who had assembled in thousands, like human vultures, in the hope of being able to loot the defeated Turks. The New Zealand Brigade quickly took up posts all round the place, and commenced "potting" at the Arabs (mostly with Turkish rifles and ammunition), who quickly faded away to a safe distance. One mounted rifleman was very keen to try his hand at shelling them with one of the captured field guns, but his officer prevented him from doing so, as there seemed more chance of his blowing himself up than anyone else.

Besides the five thousand prisoners, guns and machine-guns, the captures at Ziza included three complete trains, and a mass of other material, mostly grain, medical stores, and ammunition. The Turks were in a bad way with disease, many dead and dying lying all over the railway yard, and under trucks. The only water available was that from a stagnant reservoir with a dead man and mule lying in it; the boilers of the three engines at the station had already been drunk dry by the sick.

This final round-up at Ziza completed the work to be done on the right flank, so the New Zealand Brigade commenced its trek westward again, arriving at Jericho four days after leaving Ziza. The excitement of the operations over, many men collapsed daily from malaria. It was a pitiful sight on every day's march to see men lying in the dust as the column moved by, being given what rough attention was possible by a comrade. Others stuck grimly to their saddles, reeling with sickness, only to collapse helplessly on the ground when the day's march was ended. The night before reaching Jericho the Brigade bivouacked at Shunet Nimrin, under the foothills of Gilead, on a stony area thick with thorny scrub. A hundred and ninety men went down with malaria they had been fighting against for days, and lay about under the shelter of the bushes till they could be carted away to hospital in motor lorries called into use to supplement the shortage of ambulances.

When Jericho was reached there were barely enough men to lead all the horses. Nearly every survivor had to look after three or four, so that with such increased duties the strain on all hands was considerable.

After two or three days at Jericho, the long column of horsemen moved out once more, in a haze of white dust, for Jerusalem. Marching up the old Jericho road, the New Zealanders had their last glimpse of the Jordan Valley, where they had had such a gruelling time and lost so many of their pals from disease. Stopping one night at Talat Ed Dum en route, the Brigade halted for midday "boil-up" next day on the shoulder of the Mount of Olives, near Bethany. Then they rode down into the Valley of Jehosophat for the last time, past the Garden of Gethsemane, up round the old walls and then through the streets of Jerusalem, past the Jaffa Gate, on to the Hebron road. There they went into bivouac about a mile from the Holy City.

Three days were spent in bivouac for rest and refitting, while a last chance was afforded the New Zealanders of seeing the surroundings amongst which Christ moved in the flesh. Most of the men, however, were too tired out for sight seeing, and only too glad to take what chances of rest came to them between their duties.

Leaving Jerusalem for the last time, the New

Zealand Brigade threaded its way down the winding road towards the coast, and in two days' march had left the Hills of Judea for ever for the rolling country of the plains, going into bivouac on the ground occupied many months before near the Jewish village of Richon Le Zion. At this time it was computed that of approximately five thousand men of the New Zealand Expeditionary Force in Egypt and Palestine, something like three thousand were either in hospital or convalescent depôts, mostly with malaria.

A huge total of prisoners was taken in these final operations by the British, and although, as usual, the New Zealanders were not "in the limelight" as were the troops that reached Damascus, it has been shown that our men accomplished work of as great importance on the right flank. When, soon after reaching Richon, word came of the Armistice, the New Zealanders knew that the campaign had been brought to a victorious conclusion by their brilliant Commander-in-Chief, General Sir Edmund Allenby.

* * * * *

The Author regrets that he has been unable to obtain the figures giving the casualties of the New Zealand Mounted Rifle Brigade from the inception to the close of the Sinai-Palestine Campaign. The figures given below, as supplied by the courtesy of the Officer-in-Charge Base

Records, are the casualties of the three Mounted Regiments for the War period, and give some indication of their heavy losses as fighting units in the Empire's cause.

Auckland Mounted Rifles.

Officers.—Killed, 17; died of wounds, 6; dead —cause unknown, 1; wounded, 49. Total, 73.

Other Ranks. — Killed, 177; died of wounds, 83; died of disease, 49; dead—cause unknown, 49; drowned, 5; wounded, 645. Total, 1,008.

Wellington Mounted Rifles.

Officers.—Killed, 13; died of wounds, 9; died of disease, 3; wounded, 46. Total, 71.

Other Ranks. — Killed, 192; died of wounds, 74; died of disease, 47; dead — cause unknown, 1; drowned, 1; wounded, 685. Total, 1,000.

Canterbury Mounted Rifles.

Officers.—Killed, 15; died of wounds, 7; died of disease, 3; wounded, 50. Total, 75.

Other Ranks. — Killed, 158; died of wounds, 84; died of disease, 62; dead—cause unknown, 43; prisoner, 1; wounded, 679. Total, 1,027.

CHAPTER XX.

The Brigade remained in bivouac at Richon until a few days before Christmas, 1918. It was during this period that the trouble over the adjoining native village of Surafend occurred. It was a regrettable affair, but since various more or less inaccurate accounts of it have appeared in the press it is well that the truth should be briefly told here. Mention has been made before of the treachery of the natives — our men had suffered under this without the opportunity of redress throughout the Campaign, and the feeling against them was here to come to a head with tragic results.

Adjoining the bivouac of Richon was the village of Surafend, the natives of which indulged in constant thieving from the camps near them. One night a trooper of the New Zealand machine-gun squadron was awakened to find his kit-bag being dragged under the flap of his tent by some thief outside. He immediately arose and grappled with the native. The robber was armed with a revolver, with which he shot his assailant in the abdomen, the New Zealander shortly succumbing to a mortal wound. This outrage brought the resentment against the natives amongst the men of the

Anzac Mounted Division to fever heat. Had some drastic steps been taken immediately by the authorities to bring the murderer to book further tragedy might have been averted. What was done evidently appeared insufficient to the men by the evening of the following day, so that their anger flamed into action and resulted in their taking matters into their own hands. This they did soon after dark, when hundreds of men representing every unit in the Anzac Division, New Zealanders, Australians, and English Artillerymen, surrounded the village of Surafend. The native women and children were first put out of harm's way, and then the men, fired by hate of the people who had brought death to one of their number, entered the village, set fire to it, and clubbed the male inhabitants. A Bedouin camp situated nearby was treated in like manner, a total of thirty-eight natives being killed in vengeance for the murdered trooper.

As no evidence was forthcoming at the subsequent Court of Enquiry, the blame for this massacre could not be fixed on any individuals or section of men. As it had been to avenge the death of a New Zealander perhaps official suspicion tended to lie on the New Zealanders. The only comment that can be made in the absence of knowledge is that such a thing was inconsistent with their good record.

General Allenby paraded the entire Anzac Mounted Division, and in a short speech ''told them off." After stigmatising the men who held such a high record of achievement and honourable service in the field as murderers, he said with dramatic effect: "Once I was proud of you—I am proud of you no longer"—turned on his horse and galloped away.

Although the action of the men in thus dealing drastically with affairs themselves is morally inexcusable, it cannot be too strongly stressed that the blame for the occurrence of this regrettable incident lay, in the first instance, upon the British authorities.

The British administration all through the campaign had been weak where the natives were concerned, and had pandered to them too much. If their attitude had been different, one of firmness and punishment where it was often deserved, the natives, who have no respect for anything but the "big stick," despite anything that humanitarians may say to the contrary, would never have dared to take the liberties with the troops that they came to consider almost their right, and this tragedy would not have occurred.

The writer is aware that some readers will think the inclusion of this incident in an account like this tactless on his part, as being one of the things best left unsaid. It has been included with the idea of giving the truth to the public, who can judge for themselves rather than form their opinions from accounts distorted by bias which have appeared or may appear in the press.

While in this bivouac the Canterbury Regiment received orders to leave for a destination unknown. Horses and saddlery were handed in, and the Regiment left, with the good wishes of their comrades, to form part of the garrison of Gallipoli. Canterbury left Richon in the middle of November, before the Surafend incident, and then, shortly before Christmas, the remainder of the Brigade trekked down to Rafa and went into camp close to the scene of the historic action there.

Demobilization commenced, and some of the long-service men left for New Zealand, their places being filled by men of the last reinforcements.

All the old horses unfit for further work, some hundreds in number, were shot, to prevent their getting into the hands of the natives. This was a sad, but nevertheless humane ending of the lives of these faithful animals which had done such good work and been such trusty servants of their devoted masters. Of the remaining horses, all but a few kept for necessary work, and some that were especially valued, were handed into remount depôts.

Saddlery, Hotchkiss guns, and other gear were cleaned, greased, and returned to ordnance stores.

Canterbury Regiment returned from Gallipoli and rejoined the Brigade at Rafa at the end of January, 1919.

The New Zealanders remained at Rafa, most

of the work done being educational, until March 17th, 1919. Visions of a boat and a quick passage back to New Zealand faded away when our men heard of the outbreak of the Egyptian Rebellion. On this date they got but a few hours' notice to move, and after a hurried packing up and burning of non-essential gear, left Palestine for ever that evening in two long closely packed troop-trains for Kantara.

There they went into bivouac on the west bank of the Suez Canal for two days, while they were re-equipped to an active service footing with new gear and fresh horses. Disappointment was keen, for all hopes of an early return to New Zealand were now dashed to the ground in the prospect of many months in Egypt.

From Kantara the different units were packed off hurriedly, horses and men, in long troop trains, to various places in the Nile Delta. There they were formed into several mobile columns, each with its headquarters in a different part of the Delta. Each column was responsible for maintaining order over a large area, and for some weeks our men had a strenuous time on constant patrol work to outlying villages that showed signs of trouble. The air was tense with the excitement of a possible wholesale upheaval of the natives, which would have laid the responsibility on our men of getting all the Europeans in outlying parts into centres of safety.

One column of two hundred New Zealanders

marched out to make a reconnaissance in force to Hosh Isa, a native town of bad repute on the Senussi Frontier, where trouble was expected with hordes of Bedouins. The Royal Air Force bombed the place the night before our men went out, and this apparently acted as a deterrent to their martial spirit, for they assumed the rôle of industry at our approach and did not attempt any demonstration. In places the natives were markedly hostile and sullen, and it seemed as though any slip by those in authority would be as a match to dry grass in the conflagration that would follow.

During this time our men had a good opportunity of seeing Egypt proper and the farming life on the fertile, irrigated flats of the Delta, much interest being taken in the system of cropping followed by the natives. The principal crops grown are berseem, a forage crop not unlike lucerne, rice, cotton, maize, barley, and wheat. The country is intersected everywhere by canals, from which the water is lifted on to the land by sakhiehs or water-wheels turned by slow-moving oxen, often driven by a diminutive child.

In one town, where the troops had been compelled to inflict eighty casualties on a mob of rioting natives, one column of New Zealanders paraded through the town, a place of some fifty thousand inhabitants. As our men rode through the streets lined with people, they studied the expressions on the faces of the population —

truculence not unmixed with fear, or perhaps it might better be called discretion—that which is the better part of valour.

The natives are a cowardly lot, and were obviously cowed by our small display of armed force — though they outnumbered our men by hundreds to one.

A general uprising was averted by the prompt distribution of troops all over Egypt, and patrolling of outlying parts, and as things became quieter our men were recalled and concentrated at Ismailia, after having been about three months in the Delta.

From there they finally left for the shores of New Zealand in the Egyptian mid-summer of 1919, making the passage homewards in the two ships *Ulimaroa* and *Ellinga*.

www.ingramcontent.com/pod-product-compliance
Lightning Source LLC
Chambersburg PA
CBHW031143160426
43193CB00008B/241